THE BOOK OF FOOTBALL LISTS

Other books by Jimmy Greaves and Norman Giller

This One's on Me
The Final
The Ball Game
The Boss
The Second Half
World Cup 1930–1982
GOALS!
STOP THE GAME, I Want to Get On

THE BOOK OF FOOTBALL LISTS

JIMMY GREAVES

with Norman Giller

SIDGWICK & JACKSON
LONDON

First published in Great Britain in 1983
by Sidgwick & Jackson Limited

ISBN 0–283–99033–3 (hardcover)
ISBN 0–283–99034–1 (softcover)

Reproduced, printed and bound in Great Britain by
Hazell Watson & Viney Limited,
Aylesbury, Bucks
for Sidgwick & Jackson Limited,
1 Tavistock Chambers, Bloomsbury Way,
London WC1A 2SG

For our Shipmates
Big Al and Sweet Mary

CONTENTS

SECTION THREE: Team Selections

SECTION FOUR: Name Games

SECTION FIVE: The Poll Toppers

SECTION SIX: Top Ten Statistics

ACKNOWLEDGEMENTS

The authors wish to thank the compilers of the following books which were top of our list for reference checks:

The Rothmans Football League Players Records A to Z, compiled by Barry J. Hugman (Rothmans Publications Ltd); *Rothmans Football Yearbook*, edited by Jack Rollin (Queen Anne Press); *A Century of English International Football 1872–1972*, by Morley Farror and Douglas Lamming (Robert Hale); *Book of Football* (A Marshall Cavendish partwork); *Soccer Who's Who*, by Maurice Golesworthy (Robert Hale); *Encyclopaedia of British Football*, by Phil Soar and Martin Tyler (Marshall Cavendish).

Picture research: Malcolm Rowley

The authors and publishers would like to thank Syndicate International for the majority of the photographs that appear in this book. They would also like to thank Colorsport for photographs on pages 3, 25, 35, 75, 179, and 197 and Trinity School, New York for that on page 189.

KEY: * Alphabetical order
+ Uncapped
(E) England (S) Scotland (NI) Northern Ireland (W) Wales (Ei) Eire (Arg) Argentina (SA) South Africa (WI) West Indies

INTRODUCTION

It was an argument with my co-author, Norman Giller, that was the launching point for this book. We were driving together to a Martin Buchan testimonial dinner in Rochdale when, to pass the time, Norman started quizzing me about the greatest British players of my generation. Within a mile we were almost coming to blows because I failed to name three of 'Know-all Norm's' favourite players in my list. Being a devout coward, I said: 'Don't let's *fight* about it – let's *write* about it.' So we began to make lists of players in every category imaginable, until the selecting game became an obsession. You're now holding the result in your hand - *The Book of Football Lists*. Be warned: THIS BOOK IS DANGEROUS. If you're anything of a football fan, you won't be able to put it down once you start glancing through it. Just one list alone could cost you a night's sleep. Without looking at my selection on page 34, try picking the ten greatest players of your lifetime. I'll tell you now: it's not which players to pick that is difficult; it's deciding which players to leave out that is sheer torture.

I invited several of my football and show business friends to play the selecting game. They each selected their idea of a 'dream team'. You will find their fascinating selections sprinkled through the book and, in return for their sporting participation, I am making a donation to the National Playing Fields Association. If you're going to play the selecting game, there's just one rule to remember: each of your players must have appeared in the Football League since 1946. I hope you'll agree that this is a very select book. Now, take your pick. . .

Jimmy Greaves

SECTION ONE

TOP TEN PLAYERS

GOALKEEPERS

1940s–1950s		*1960s–1980s*	
1	**Frank Swift (E)**	1	**Pat Jennings (NI)**
2	**Jack Kelsey (W)**	2	**Gordon Banks (E)**
3	**Ted Ditchburn (E)**	3	**Peter Shilton (E)**
4	**Bert Trautmann (Ger)**	4	**Ray Clemence (E)**
5	**Bert Williams (E)**	5	**Peter Bonetti (E)**
6	**Tommy Younger (S)**	6	**Ron Springett (E)**
7	**Harry Gregg (NI)**	7	**Alex Stepney (E)**
8	**Gil Merrick (E)**	8	**Phil Parkes (E)**
9	**Sam Bartram (E)†**	9	**Bob Wilson (S)**
10	**Eddie Hopkinson (E)**	10	**Gordon West (E)**

Jimmy Greaves: I had no hesitation in making the legendary Frank Swift my No. 1 choice in the 1940s–50s list, but I anguished over having to leave out goalkeepers of the calibre of Alan Hodgkinson, George Farm, Colin McDonald and Ray Wood. The No. 1 spot in the modern list gave me the biggest headache, Pat Jennings finally pipping Gordon Banks by a fingertip. Pat got my vote because of his incredible consistency over a record stretch of more than one thousand games. Gordon was a complete master of the goal area and might have matched Pat's long-playing record but for the eye injury that cruelly brought a premature end to his career. Ronnie Simpson, Celtic's last line of defence in the 1967 European Cup winning team, narrowly missed out in both lists after a safe-handling career that spanned twenty years from the late 1940s.

FULL-BACKS

1940s–1950s

1. **Roger Byrne (E)**
2. **Don Howe (E)**
3. **Alf Ramsey (E)**
4. **Johnny Carey (Ei)**
5. **Walley Barnes (W)**
6. **Jeff Hall (E)**
7. **Laurie Scott (E)**
8. **Bill Eckersley (E)**
9. **George Hardwick (E)**
10. **Alex Parker (S)**

1960s–1980s

1. **Ray Wilson (E)**
2. **Jimmy Armfield (E)**
3. **Kenny Sansom (E)**
4. **George Cohen (E)**
5. **Terry Cooper (E)**
6. **Eddie McCreadie (S)**
7. **Derek Statham (E)**
8. **Viv Anderson (E)**
9. **Keith Newton (E)**
10. **Alex Elder (NI)**

Jimmy Greaves: Two tragic players figure prominently in my 1940s–50s list – Roger Byrne, who was a victim of the 1958 Munich air crash, and Jeff Hall, who was cut down in his prime by polio. Byrne was an artist of a left-back who – like Terry Cooper a decade later – showed all the attacking flair of a converted left-winger. At first I had Alf Ramsey in No.2 spot, but then decided that Don Howe was quicker on the turn and more mobile. I had no doubt about putting the elegant Ray Wilson at No.1 in the modern list. My old team-mate Ken Shellito, who signed for Chelsea the same day as me, would have been high in the list with his side-kick, Eddie McCreadie, but for a knee injury wrecking his career when he was at his peak. Two great Scots, George Young and Danny McGrain, would have 'walked' into the lists but neither of them played League football south of the border.

Roger Byrne, an artist of a left-back

CENTRE–HALVES

1940s–1950s		*1960–1980s*	
1	**John Charles (W)**	**1**	**Roy McFarland (E)**
2	**Neil Franklin (E)**	**2**	**Mike England (W)**
3	**Billy Wright (E)**	**3**	**Jackie Charlton (E)**
4	**Bobby Evans (S)**	**4**	**Dave Watson (E)**
5	**Ray Daniel (W)**	**5**	**Peter Swan (E)**
6	**Harry Johnston (E)**	**6**	**Charlie Hurley (Ei)**
7	**Frank Brennan (S)**	**7**	**Brian Labone (E)**
8	**Jack Froggatt (E)**	**8**	**Allan Hunter (NI)**
9	**Syd Owen (E)**	**9**	**Maurice Norman (E)**
10	**Leslie Compton (E)**	**10**	**Ron Yeats (S)**

Jimmy Greaves: Few people could argue with my choice of John Charles as No.1 centre-half in the Golden Oldies list. He was equally effective at centre-forward and would have the support of many veteran fans as the greatest footballer ever bred in Britain, even though he did flourish much of his best football in Italy, where the 'Gentle Giant' was a god. Roy McFarland was a short head winner over Mike England and Jack Charlton for the No.1 berth in the moderns list. Frank McLintock just missed out in the 1960s–80s table because I rated him a more productive player at wing-half. Gordon McQueen and Ian Ure were two other Anglo-Scots who I had reluctantly to cross off my short-list. Celtic Colossus Billy McNeill was a magnificent player, but he did not qualify for the vote because he played all his League football in Scotland.

WING-HALVES

1940s–1950s

1 **Duncan Edwards (E)**
2 **Danny Blanchflower (NI)**
3 **Ron Burgess (W)**
4 **Joe Mercer (E)**
5 **Jimmy Scoular (S)**
6 **Billy Wright (E)**
7 **Bobby Robson**
8 **Bill Slater (E)**
9 **Tommy Docherty (S)**
=10 **Ronnie Clayton (E)**
Jimmy Dickinson (E)

1960s–1980s

1 **Dave Mackay (S)**
2 **Bryan Robson (E)**
3 **Graeme Souness (S)**
4 **Pat Crerand (S)**
5 **Billy Bremner (S)**
6 **Nobby Stiles (E)**
7 **Frank McLintock (S)**
8 **Gordon Milne (E)**
9 **Bobby Robson (E)**
10 **Emlyn Hughes (E)**

Jimmy Greaves: You don't hear players called wing-halves any more but they still exist in everything but name. Bryan Robson is typical of the breed, a dynamo in midfield who lifts and inspires the players around him by the sheer force and power of his own performances. He is carrying on the tradition set by magnificent powerhouse players like my old Spurs team-mate, Dave Mackay, and the devastating Duncan Edwards, who – a quarter of a century after his tragic death in the Munich air disaster – is still considered by many people inside the game to have been the finest all-round footballer ever produced in England. Billy Wright features in my 1940s–50s list at wing-half as well as at centre-half. He was a dynamic right-half with Wolves and England before switching to the middle of the defence. It was a toss-up between my old Spurs team-mate, Alan Mullery, and Emlyn Hughes for 10th spot in the modern list, Emlyn just getting the edge because of his better finishing power.

Duncan Edwards, the perfect all-rounder

BILLY WRIGHT'S DREAM TEAM

1 Gordon Banks
2 Jimmy Armfield
3 Roger Byrne
4 Danny Blanchflower (capt)
5 Neil Franklin
6 Duncan Edwards
7 Stanley Matthews
8 Wilf Mannion
9 John Charles
10 Bobby Charlton
11 Tom Finney
Sub: Dave Mackay

'George Best and Kenny Dalglish were on my original short-list, but I decided the way round that problem was to stick to players who were in action in my era. It cost me sleep leaving out players of the quality of Tommy Lawton and Raich Carter, and also all those magnificent team-mates of mine in the Wolves side of the Stan Cullis days. This is my "dream team" but it gave me nightmares selecting it!'

Billy Wright is one of football's all-time favourites. He skippered the great Wolves side of the 1950s and captained England 90 times while winning 105 caps. Billy is now an executive with Central Television.

Billy Wright (right), one of football's all-time favourites

CENTRAL DEFENDERS

1 Bobby Moore (E)
2 Dave Mackay (S)
3 Norman Hunter (E)
4 Colin Todd (E)
5 Martin Buchan (S)
6 Alan Hansen (S)
7 Ron Flowers (E)
8 Kevin Beattie (E)
9 Phil Thompson (E)
10 David O'Leary (Ei)

Jimmy Greaves: Bobby Moore brought composure and control to the heart of any defence in which he played. He lacked authority in the air and was not the quickest thing on two legs, but his positioning sense was so acute that he rarely looked stretched. Lion-hearted Dave Mackay switched from the traditional wing-half role to the centre of the defence when he moved from Spurs to Derby, and was an instant master in the new role. All the players listed in this Top Ten list were not only sound defensively but could put sudden pressure on the opposition with imaginatively placed passes out of defence.

MIDFIELD MAESTROS

1940s–1950s

1. **Raich Carter (E)**
2. **Johnny Haynes (E)**
3. **Jimmy McIlroy (NI)**
4. **Peter Doherty (NI)**
5. **Wilf Mannion (E)**
6. **Len Shackleton (E)**
7. **Eddie Baily (E)**
8. **Bobby Collins (S)**
9. **Ivor Allchurch (W)**
10. **Peter Broadbent (E)**

1960s–1980s

1. **Colin Bell (E)**
2. **Liam Brady (Ei)**
3. **Martin Peters (E)**
4. **Trevor Brooking (E)**
5. **George Eastham (E)**
6. **Glenn Hoddle (E)**
7. **Johnny Giles (Ei)**
8. **Bobby Charlton (E)**
9. **Alan Ball (E)**
10. **Osvaldo Ardiles (Arg)**

Jimmy Greaves: These are the pass masters of football, the players who dictate the pace and pattern of matches. Raich Carter tops my Golden Oldies list because he was a tactical genius. Johnny Haynes was the best passer of a ball I ever played with and I consider myself lucky to have been on the receiving end. John White, the 'Ghost of White Hart Lane', would have been a certainty for my list but for being cut down in his prime by a bolt of lightning. 'Slim Jim' Baxter was another Scot who was on my short-list, but I finally crossed him off because he never really produced his magical best in the Football League.

Tom Finney, a flying winger

WING WIZARDS

1940s–1950s		*1960s–1980s*	
1	**Tom Finney (E)**	**1**	**George Best (NI)**
2	**Stanley Matthews (E)**	**2**	**Jimmy Johnstone (S)**
3	**Billy Liddell (S)**	**3**	**John Robertson (S)**
4	**Bobby Charlton (E)**	**4**	**Peter Thompson (E)**
5	**Cliff Jones (W)**	**5**	**Steve Coppell (E)**
6	**Bryan Douglas (E)**	**6**	**John Connelly (E)**
7	**Jimmy Mullen (E)**	**7**	**Ian Callaghan (E)**
8	**Johnny Hancocks (E)**	**8**	**Terry Paine (E)**
9	**Peter McParland (NI)**	**9**	**Peter Lorimer (S)**
10	**Billy Bingham (NI)**	**10**	**Peter Barnes (E)**

Jimmy Greaves: Wingers became scarce in the late 1960s and through the 1970s, but we had the magic of George Best and the skills of Jimmy Johnstone to remind us of the 'Golden Age' of Matthews and Finney. They have started to come back into fashion with shining black pearls like Mark Chamberlain and John Barnes leading the way. For the spectators, there are few more exciting sights in football than a winger jinking Matthews-style past full-backs and crossing the ball into the middle. It's my personal view that Bobby Charlton was at his most devastating when operating as an out-and-out winger for Manchester United and England. Finney ahead of Matthews? It's an age-old debating point in football and most pros I talk to agree that Tom just gets the nod because he played with more purpose.

GOAL MERCHANTS

1940s–1950s		*1960s–1980s*	
1	**Stan Mortensen (E)**	**1**	**Denis Law (S)**
2	**Brian Clough (E)**	**3**	**Kenny Dalglish (S)**
3	**Nat Lofthouse (E)**	**3**	**Roger Hunt (E)**
4	**Dennis Viollet (E)**	**4**	**Trevor Francis (E)**
5	**Billy Liddell (S)**	**5**	**Geoff Hurst (E)**
6	**Stan Pearson (E)**	**6**	**Allan Clarke (E)**
7	**Arthur Rowley (E)†**	**7**	**Bryan (Pop) Robson (E)†**
8	**John Atyeo (E)**	**8**	**Mike Channon (E)**
9	**Ronnie Allen (E)**	**9**	**Francis Lee (E)**
10	**Jackie Mudie (S)**	**10**	**Ray Crawford (E)**

Jimmy Greaves: As goals were always my business, I found these lists particularly difficult to compile. There were so many strikers that I have admired and they were all battling for a place on my memory screen. In my Golden Oldies list, the likes of Len Shackleton, Raich Carter and Wilf Mannion were as much schemers as scorers, and this is why they did not make the Top Ten. You may be surprised to find Kevin Keegan missing from my moderns list but I consider Kevin a busy, buzzing utility type of player able to adapt to any role. He has never been a really prolific goal scorer, although he was leading First Division marksman in 1981–1982. The one certainly was Denis 'The Electric Heel' Law taking the No. 1 spot, with Kenny Dalglish just pipping Roger Hunt, his predecessor in the Liverpool firing line, for second place.

Stan Mortensen, the 'Blackpool Bomber'

TOMMY STEELE'S DREAM TEAM

1 Gordon Banks
2 Walley Barnes
3 Bobby Thomson
4 Nobby Stiles
5 Bobby Moore (capt)
6 Duncan Edwards
7 Stanley Matthews
8 Denis Law
9 Tommy Lawton
10 Bobby Charlton
11 George Best
Sub: Bryan Robson

‘My team, although strong and knowledgeable at the back, is picked to attack, attack and attack again. Football should be about winning not containing. It needs to be a game of style rather than rush and, above all, it has to be founded on talent and hard work. With a hearty midfield and a forward line lethal in all departments, how can this team lose?’

Tommy Steele had the ability to make it as a professional footballer, but chose instead a show business career that has now stretched for more than twenty years as a top-flight star. He has strong, positive views on football and it was the game's loss when he failed in a bid to become chairman of Millwall.

CENTRE–FORWARDS

1940s–1950s		*1960s–1980s*	
1	**Tommy Lawton (E)**	**1**	**Bobby Smith (E)**
2	**Nat Lofthouse (E)**	**2**	**Malcolm Macdonald (E)**
3	**John Charles (W)**	**3**	**Johnny Byrne (E)**
4	**Jackie Milburn (E)**	**4**	**Ron Davies (W)**
5	**Tom Finney (E)**	**5**	**Brian Clough (E)**
6	**Tommy Taylor (E)**	**6**	**Ian St John (S)**
7	**Jack Rowley (E)**	**7**	**Derek Dougan (NI)**
8	**Trevor Ford (W)**	**8**	**Jeff Astle (E)**
9	**Roy Bentley (E)**	**9**	**Alan Gilzean (S)**
10	**Ronnie Allen (E)**	**10**	**Ray Crawford (E)**

Jimmy Greaves: The 1940s–50s list almost picked itself. I went for the traditional, blood and thunder spearheads which meant there was no place for that subtle, deep-lying master Don Revie. The modern list gave me much more trouble, as a procession of superb No.9s queued for a place in my memory. Brian Clough, my side-kick in his two England appearances, might have got higher but for a knee injury forcing him into premature retirement. I juggled with lists that at one time included Martin Chivers, Peter Osgood, Alex Young, Joe Royle, Paul Mariner, Peter Withe, Derek Kevan, Cyrille Regis, Joe Baker and Joe Jordan before finally settling for this Top Ten. Scotland's Colin Stein was one of my favourite centre-forwards but he never really did himself justice in the English League after joining Coventry from Rangers, for whom he had been a devastating player.

THE TOP TEN CAPTAINS' TABLE

1. **Danny Blanchflower (NI)**
2. **Dave Mackay (S)**
3. **Billy Wright (E)**
4. **Joe Mercer (E)**
5. **Billy Bremner (S)**
6. **Joe Harvey (E)**
7. **Frank McLintock (S)**
8. **Bobby Moore (E)**
9. **Ron Yeats (S)**
10. **John McGovern (S)**

Jimmy Greaves: I was privileged to play under two of the greatest captains that ever tossed a coin during my time with Spurs. Danny Blanchflower was a tactical genius who dictated the pace and pattern of matches by putting his superior mind to work and directing the flow of play with a stream of intelligent orders. Dave Mackay inspired the players around him by his tremendous physical presence and his buccaneering competitive spirit. There are five Scots in my Top Ten list, which is testimony to the natural leadership qualities that so many Scots possess.

Danny Blanchflower, a tactical genius

TEN SHARP SHOOTERS WHO PACKED DYNAMITE IN THEIR BOOTS

1. **Peter Lorimer (S)**
2. **Frank Neary (E)†**
3. **Ted Phillips (E)†**
4. **Jack Rowley (E)**
5. **Cliff Holton (E)†**
6. **David Herd (S)**
7. **Duncan Edwards (E)**
8. **Tommy Lawton (E)**
9. **Bobby Charlton (E)**
10. **Bobby Smith (E)**

Jimmy Greaves: You may not have heard of Frank Neary, but his shooting power is still talked about with awe by the old pros who were around in the 1950s. Frank had thighs like a Tour de France cyclist and could hit the back of the net from the half-way line. Ted Phillips was a smash shot with Alf Ramsey's championship-winning Ipswich team, and Cliff Holton made nets bulge for a queue of clubs including Arsenal, Watford and Northampton.

Tommy Lawton, putting Scotland's defence under pressure

TEN HEADMASTERS WHO WERE ACES IN THE AIR

1 **Tommy Lawton (E)**
2 **Ron Davies (W)**
3 **Nat Lofthouse (E)**
4 **Tommy Taylor (E)**
5 **John Charles (W)**
6 **Tony Hateley (E)†**
7 **Jeff Astle (E)**
8 **Joe Royle (E)**
9 **Denis Law (S)**
10 **Cliff Jones (W)**

Jimmy Greaves: They are all centre-forwards with the exception of Denis Law and Cliff Jones. Denis was a great 'climber' who had the gift of being able to hang in the air as if suspended by an invisible rope. Cliffie Jones was the bravest header of a ball I have ever seen. He was only a lightweight but could rise like a salmon at the far post to head vital goals. Tommy Lawton was without question the greatest header of a ball in post-war football. He headed several goals from *outside* the penalty area during his power-packed career.

THE TEN PLAYERS MOST LIKELY TO PUT 10,000 ON THE GATE

1 George Best
2 Stanley Matthews
3 Bobby Charlton
4 Len Shackleton
5 Tom Finney
6 Denis Law
7 Tommy Lawton
8 Jackie Milburn
9 Kevin Keegan
10 Raich Carter

Jimmy Greaves: These are the players I rate as the ten top crowd pullers in post-war British football; the men the fans would dig deepest into their pockets to see. They all have one thing in common – they put entertainment high on their list of priorities. Jimmy Johnstone, Rodney Marsh, Peter Osgood, Charlie George and Peter Doherty were also king entertainers, but not quite in the class of my Top Ten players as turnstile turners.

DICK FRANCIS'S DREAM TEAM

1 Gordon Banks
2 George Cohen
3 Ray Wilson
4 Nobby Stiles
5 Billy Wright (capt)
6 Joe Mercer
7 Stanley Matthews
8 Stan Mortensen
9 Tommy Lawton
10 Bobby Charlton
11 Tom Finney
Sub: Bobby Moore

‘I find writing novels easier work than trying to select football teams! After wrestling with the memories of so many outstanding players, I turned to my son Felix for help and this is the combination we settled on. We feel it would be a difficult team to beat. Win, lose or draw, they would provide a lot of pleasure and entertainment for the spectators.’

Dick Francis, former top steeplechase jockey, is now one of the world's foremost thriller writers.

Kevin Keegan, a crowd-pulling player, in action against Hungary

THE TEN MOST-FEARED TACKLERS

1 Norman Hunter (E)
2 Jimmy Scoular (S)
3 Dave Mackay (S)
4 Ron Harris (E)†
5 Tommy Smith (E)
6 Peter Storey (E)
7 Nobby Stiles (E)
8 Duncan Edwards (E)
9 Maurice Setters (E)†
10 Billy Bremner (S)

Jimmy Greaves: All of these players autographed my shins at one time or another, and I can vouch that each of them had a tackle like a clap of thunder. Old-timers tell me that Wilf Copping was the hardest tackling player of all time. Thank goodness, he was before *my* time. Wilf used to play for Leeds and Arsenal, where his tradition of toughness was carried on in grand style by Norman Hunter and Peter Storey. Duncan Edwards *looked* the most powerful of all these hard men. He was built like an oak tree and ran through opponents as if they weren't there.

Norman Hunter, the man with the leg-biting tackle

THE TEN HARDEST PLAYERS TO CATCH

1 Barry Bridges (E)
2 Jackie Milburn (E)
3 Cliff Jones (W)
4 Steve Heighway (Ei)
5 Malcolm Macdonald (E)
6 Billy Liddell (S)
7 Tom Finney (E)
8 George Best (NI)
9 Stan Mortensen (E)
10 Peter Thompson (E)

Jimmy Greaves: These were the fast men of football. Barry Bridges was a schoolboy sprint champion and could maintain top speed over long distances. The rest of the players in my list were untouchable over short distances. Sudden acceleration was a prominent part of their game. Jackie Milburn was christened John Edward Thompson Milburn – and more than lived up to his JET initials. Funnily enough *the* fastest footballer was probably a goalkeeper: Scottish international Bobby Ferguson, who won a professional footballers' sprint championship while with West Ham.

THE TEN GREATEST BALL PLAYERS

1. **David Burnside (E)†**
2. **Tommy Harmer (E)†**
3. **Len Shackleton (E)**
4. **Stanley Matthews (E)**
5. **Rodney Marsh (E)**
6. **George Best (NI)**
7. **Johnny Byrne (E)**
8. **Charlie Cooke (S)**
9. **Wilf Mannion (E)**
10. **Peter Osgood (E)**

Jimmy Greaves: All of these players were complete masters of ball control. They could make the ball sit up and beg, and could take on and beat any defender in man-to-man situations. It's a sad fact of footballing life that every one of them at some stage in his career had to face the criticism of being greedy or a luxury. Yes, even the great Stanley Matthews was sometimes accused of hogging the ball. David Burnside was a magnificent juggler of the ball who used to go on stage giving exhibitions. Unfortunately he lacked the necessary vision to harness his great skills to a team pattern, and he never reached his true potential. Tommy 'The Charmer' Harmer had immaculate skill but it was a lack of physical strength rather than ability that prevented him going beyond his stage at Spurs to the international honours he deserved.

THE TEN CHIP KINGS*

1 **Eddie Baily (E)**
2 **Danny Blanchflower (NI)**
3 **Liam Brady (Ei)**
4 **Johnny Byrne (E)**
5 **Bobby Collins (S)**
6 **Peter Doherty (NI)**
7 **Johnny Giles (Ei)**
8 **Wilf Mannion (E)**
9 **Rodney Marsh (E)**
10 **Len Shackleton (E)**

Jimmy Greaves: The chip pass or chip shot is becoming a lost art. These ten players were masters of the chip and could use their feet like number nine golf irons. I recall Eddie Baily once chipping a corner-kick against the back of the referee and then chipping the rebound to the far post, where Len Duquemin headed a spectacular goal for Spurs. The ref' didn't know what was going on and let the goal stand. It was a typical piece of Cockney cheek from the effervescent Baily. I also remember Johnny 'Budgie' Byrne chipping a last-minute goal against Portugal in Lisbon to complete a hat-trick, and the one and only Shack scored the greatest goal of his memorable career at Wembley when he chipped the ball over the West German goalkeeper's head in a 1954 international match. It is no coincidence that all the players listed here have strong personalities. You have got to have a lot of nerve and confidence as well as skill to perform the chip shot or pass in the heat of battle. Glen Hoddle and Ray Wilkins are the most accomplished 'chip artists' in the 1980s' England squad.

Eddie Baily, master of the chip

BOBBY CHARLTON'S DREAM TEAM

1 Bert Trautmann
2 Jimmy Armfield
3 Ray Wilson
4 Bobby Moore (capt)
5 John Charles
6 Duncan Edwards
7 Stanley Matthews
8 Danny Blanchflower
9 Denis Law
10 George Best
11 Tom Finney
Sub: Kenny Dalglish

'I tried many permutations before arriving at this team. It was really difficult leaving out so many players that I have admired over the years. If those I've not chosen never speak to me again, it will all be down to Jimmy Greaves. Thanks a lot, Jim! Notice that I have selected conventional wingers. It makes for the best spectacle.'

Bobby Charlton, capped 106 times, has been England's greatest footballing ambassador and remains one of the most popular and respected figures in the game. He was an influential member of England's 1966 World Cup winning team and skippered the Manchester United side that captured the European Cup in 1968.

Bobby Charlton (left), England's greatest footballing ambassador, duels for the ball with tough tackling Maurice Setters

TEN GREAT PLAY-ANYWHERE PLAYERS

1 Paul Madeley (E)

He could fit into any position for Leeds United and play like a master. Paul was happiest in defence but was also an accomplished attacking player. He wore shirt numbers two, three, five, six, eight, and eleven while winning twenty-four caps for England

2 Martin Peters (E)

He was such a man of all parts at West Ham that he wore ten different numbers, including once filling in as emergency goalkeeper. Martin liked a 'free' role in midfield and was devastating at coming through on blind-side runs into the penalty area. It was his all-round ability that inspired Alf Ramsey's famous quote: 'Peters is ten years ahead of his time'

Martin Peters (left), ten years ahead of his time

3 Duncan Edwards (E)

Nobody really found out Duncan's best position before his tragic death in the Munich air disaster. He was a commanding player in the back line and in midfield, and also had an eye for a half chance in the penalty area

4 John Charles (W)

Big John was equally menacing whether leading the attack or standing like a Welsh mountain in the middle of the defence. He was a prolific goalscorer and was also a redoubtable 'stopper' centre-half

5 John Hewie (S)

This tall, lithe South African-born Scot played in nine different positions for Charlton, including goal. He was at his best at full-back and wore the Scottish number three shirt sixteen times, and also won caps in the two wing-half positions

6 Jack Froggatt (E)

He was capped for England in such contrasting positions as centre-half and left-winger. Jack was a key man in the Portsmouth team that won two successive League championships in the immediate post-war years

7 Tom Finney (E)

Tom filled four different forward positions for England. He was one of the 'Great Untouchables' on either wing and yet many people rated centre-forward the place that suited him best

8 Ray Kennedy (E)

He was an out-and-out striker with the Arsenal 'double' team of 1970–71, forming a goal-snatching partnership with John Radford. On his move to Liverpool, Ray became one of the League's outstanding left-sided midfield players

9 Billy Liddell (S)

He was such an intoxicating influence at Anfield that during his reign as King of the Kop the club became known as 'Liddellpool'. Though at his most lethal on the left wing, Billy could bomb defences from all five front-line positions

10 Johnny Carey (Ei)

This affable Irishman joined Manchester United as an inside-forward in 1938, and during the next fifteen years played in ten different positions for the Old Trafford club. He finally specialized at right-back, from where he skippered the United team that won the 1948 FA Cup in such regal style

IDENTIKIT OF THE PERFECT FORWARD

1 The shooting power and accuracy of **Peter Lorimer**
2 The ball control of **George Best**
3 The heading ability of **Tommy Lawton**
4 The penalty area reactions and reflexes of **Denis Law**
5 The finishing instincts of **Jimmy Greaves****
6 The physique of **John Charles**
7 The change of pace of **Stanley Matthews**
8 The passing precision of **Johnny Haynes**
9 The poise and balance of **Bobby Charlton**
10 The heart and all-round ability of **TOM FINNEY**

**Editor's selection

IDENTIKIT OF THE PERFECT DEFENDER

1 The tackling power of **Norman Hunter**
2 The heading ability of **John Charles**
3 The determination and tenacity of **Nobby Stiles**
4 The composure of **Bobby Moore**
5 The drive of **Billy Wright**
6 The physical presence of **Dave Mackay**
7 The recovery powers of **Jimmy Armfield**
8 The poise and passing of **Neil Franklin**
9 The attacking instincts of **Terry Cooper**
10 The all-round ability of **DUNCAN EDWARDS**

IDENTIKIT OF THE PERFECT GOALKEEPER

1 The catching skill of **Peter Bonetti**
2 The awareness of **Jack Kelsey**
3 The physical presence of **Frank Swift**
4 The reflexes of **Gordon Banks**
5 The composure of **Peter Shilton**
6 The positional sense of **Ray Clemence**
7 The agility of **Bert Trautmann**
8 The goal-area authority of **Bert Williams**
9 The committed attitude of **Ron Springett**
10 The all-round ability of **PAT JENNINGS**

IDENTIKIT OF THE PERFECT MANAGER

1 The commonsense of **Bob Paisley**
2 The confidence of **Brian Clough**
3 The flair of **Malcolm Allison**
4 The honesty of **Bill Nicholson**
5 The public relations of **Joe Mercer**
6 The positive attitude of **Bill Shankly**
7 The enthusiasm of **Bobby Robson**
8 The total commitment of **Stan Cullis**
9 The tactical genius of **Alf Ramsey**
10 The all-round ability of **MATT BUSBY**

JOHN CONTEH'S DREAM TEAM

1 Gordon Banks
2 Jimmy Armfield
3 Ray Wilson
4 Danny Blanchflower (capt)
5 John Charles
6 Duncan Edwards
7 George Best
8 Kenny Dalglish
9 Billy Liddell
10 Bobby Charlton
11 Tom Finney
Sub: Kevin Keegan

‘I contend that this team has got that vital ingredient – perfect balance. Every man would have total command of the area involved with his position. Each player would be capable of holding, carrying or moving the ball with perfectly-placed passes, and the men at the back would be able to turn defence to attack very swiftly. With this forward line, no half chance would go begging. For me it really *is* a dream of a team.’

John Conteh, former world light-heavyweight boxing champion, is a good-quality footballer and – of course – a Liverpool fan.

THE TEN GREATEST BRITISH PLAYERS OF MY LIFETIME*

1. **George Best (NI)**
2. **Raich Carter (E)**
3. **John Charles (W)**
4. **Duncan Edwards (E)**
5. **Tom Finney (E)**
6. **Denis Law (S)**
7. **Tommy Lawton (E)**
8. **Dave Mackay (S)**
9. **Stanley Matthews (E)**
10. **Bobby Moore (E)**

Jimmy Greaves: I have placed them in alphabetical order because there is no way I could separate them. Each was a genius in his own right. If a gun was placed to my head I would select George Best as the greatest of them all. He had *everything.* Duncan Edwards was cut down before he had reached his peak, but I feel he would have developed into a player on the Pele scale, a star admired and applauded around the world. I can tell you that if I had been asked to name my top dozen, Bobby Charlton and Danny Blanchflower were the next two names on my list. Kenny Dalglish was the only present-day player who came into my considerations. Now you try to select *your* ten lifetime greats. I warn you now – it'll put years on you when it comes to which players to leave out!

George Best, a player who had everything

SECTION TWO

TOP TEN GENERAL

THE TEN MANAGERS MOST ABLE TO MANAGE

1 Matt Busby (Manchester United)

League championship 1951–52, 1955–56, 1956–57, 1964–65, 1966–67; runners-up 1946–47, 1947–48, 1948–49, 1950–51, 1958–59, 1963–64, 1967–68. FA Cup winners 1948, 1963; runners-up 1957, 1958. European Cup semi-finalists 1957, 1958, 1966, 1969; champions 1968

2 Bob Paisley (Liverpool)

League championship 1975–76, 1976–77, 1978–79, 1979–80, 1981–82, 1982–83; runners-up 1974–75, 1977–78. FA Cup runners-up 1977. League Cup winners 1981, 1982, 1983; runners-up 1978. European Cup champions 1977, 1978, 1981. UEFA Cup winners 1976

3 Bill Shankly (Liverpool)

League championship 1963–64, 1965–66, 1972–73; runners-up 1968–69, 1973–74. Second Division champions 1961–62. FA Cup winners 1965, 1974; runners-up 1971. European Cup Winners' Cup runners-up 1966. UEFA Cup winners 1973

4 Alf Ramsey (Ipswich Town and England)

League championship 1961–62. Second Division champions 1960–61. Third Division (South) champions 1956–57. England manager: World Cup winners 1966

5 Bill Nicholson (Spurs)

League championship 1960–61; runners-up 1962–63. FA Cup winners 1961, 1962, 1967. League Cup winners 1971, 1973. European Cup semi-finalists 1962. European Cup Winners' Cup winners 1963. UEFA Cup winners 1972

6 Brian Clough (Derby County and Nottingham Forest)

League championship 1971–72, 1974–75. Second Division champions 1968–69. With Forest: League championship 1977–78; runners-up 1978–79. Second Division: promoted third place 1976–77. Football League Cup winners 1978, 1979; runners-up 1980. European Cup champions 1979, 1980

7 Stan Cullis (Wolves)

League championship 1953–54, 1957–58, 1958–59; runners-up 1949–50, 1954–55, 1959–60. FA Cup winners 1949, 1960

8 Arthur Rowe (Spurs)

League championship 1950–51; runners-up 1951–52. Second Division champions 1949–50

9 Don Revie (Leeds United)

League championship 1968–69, 1973–74; runners-up 1964–65, 1965–66, 1969–70, 1970–71, 1971–72. Second Division champions 1963–64. FA Cup winners 1972; runners-up 1965, 1970, 1973. League Cup winners 1968. European Cup Winners' Cup runners-up 1973. Fairs Cup winners 1969, 1971; runners-up 1967

10 Joe Mercer (Manchester City)

League championship 1967–68. Second Division champions 1965–66. FA Cup winners 1969. League Cup winners 1970. European Cup Winners' Cup winners 1970

Jimmy Greaves: If I had been including the Scottish League in my considerations, Jock Stein would have been up there challenging for No.1 position following his exploits with Celtic. The record for each manager speaks for itself. At one stage I had Bill Shankly above Bob Paisley in No. 2 spot because he left a foundation on which Bob could build. But Paisley's stunning consistency right up to the 1982–83 season of his retirement inched him ahead of his old boss Shanks. Most of these managers worked in harness with a trusted right-hand man – Matt Busby (Jimmy Murphy), Alf Ramsey (Harold Shepherdson), Bill Nicholson (Eddie Baily), Arthur Rowe (Jimmy Anderson), Don Revie (Les Cocker), Joe Mercer (Malcolm Allison) and Brian Clough (Peter Taylor). I would like to have seen Bob Paisley stay at Anfield for just one more season to see if he could have matched Herbert Chapman's remarkable hat-trick of League championship victories with Arsenal (1933–34–35).

SIR MATT BUSBY'S DREAM TEAM

1 Frank Swift
2 Johnny Carey
3 Roger Byrne
4 Danny Blanchflower
5 Jackie Charlton
6 Duncan Edwards
7 Tom Finney
8 Bobby Charlton
9 Tommy Taylor
10 Denis Law
11 George Best
Sub: Dave Mackay

'It was my business to select football teams for more than twenty-five years and I have to confess that this was the hardest one of all to pick. I was fortunate enough to have been associated in one way or another with just about every great player you can put your mind to, and it was tremendously difficult deciding which ones to leave out. I finally went for this balanced combination and the team's strength can be measured by the fact that the great Dave Mackay is on the substitute's bench. You will notice that I have not nominated a captain. With this team there would be eleven captains on the field. Yes, it's certainly a manager's *dream* team.'

Sir Matt Busby's remarkable managerial triumphs with Manchester United are chronicled on page 36. He was also an outstanding player, driving the Manchester City team of the 1930's to two successive FA Cup Finals form his position at right-half. He later featured in midfield for Liverpool and was a Scottish international.

Sir Matt Busby, the No. 1 manager

TEN GREAT PLAYERS WHO FOUND IT DIFFICULT TO MANAGE*

1 **Alan Ball**
Appointed player-manager of Blackpool 1980. Sacked 1981

2 **Bobby Charlton**
Appointed Preston manager 1973. Resigned 1975 following a dispute with his directors over a transfer deal

3 **George Hardwick**
Appointed manager of Sunderland 1964. Dismissed 1965. Later had two years in charge at Gateshead

4 **Johnny Haynes**
Appointed Fulham manager 1968. Resigned 1968

5 **Geoff Hurst**
Appointed Chelsea manager 1979. Sacked 1981

6 **Stanley Matthews**
Appointed Port Vale general manager 1965. Resigned 1969

7 **Frank McLintock**
Appointed Leicester City manager 1977. Resigned 1978

8 **Jackie Milburn**
Appointed Ipswich Town manager 1963. Resigned 1964

9 **Martin Peters**
Appointed Sheffield United manager 1980. Resigned 1981

10 **Nobby Stiles**
Appointed Preston manager 1977. Resigned 1981

TEN GREAT MANAGERS WHO NEVER PLAYED REGULAR FIRST DIVISION FOOTBALL*

1 **Malcolm Allison**
Clubs: Charlton Athletic and West Ham

2 **Ron Atkinson**
Clubs: Aston Villa and Oxford United

3 **Keith Burkinshaw**
Clubs: Liverpool, Workington, Scunthorpe

4 **Lawrie McMenemy**
Clubs: Newcastle and Gateshead

5 **Bertie Mee**
Club: Derby County

6 **Ron Saunders**
Clubs: Everton, Tonbridge, Gillingham, Portsmouth, Watford, Charlton Athletic

7 **Dave Sexton**
Clubs: Luton, West Ham, Leyton Orient, Brighton, Crystal Palace

8 **Alec Stock**
Clubs: Charlton Athletic, QPR, Yeovil Town

9 **Graham Taylor**
Clubs: Grimsby and Lincoln City

10 **Tony Waddington**
Clubs: Manchester United (amateur), Crewe Alexandra

THE POSITIONS TEN GREAT MANAGERS FILLED AS PLAYERS*

1 **Matt Busby** (right-half)
2 **Brian Clough** (centre-forward)
3 **Stan Cullis** (centre-half)
4 **Joe Mercer** (left-half)
5 **Bill Nicholson** (right-half)
6 **Bob Paisley** (left-half)
7 **Alf Ramsey** (right-back)
8 **Don Revie** (centre-forward)
9 **Arthur Rowe** (centre-half)
10 **Bill Shankly** (right-half)

TOM FINNEY'S DREAM TEAM

1 **Gordon Banks**
2 **Laurie Scott**
3 **Ray Wilson**
4 **Bobby Moore (capt)**
5 **Neil Franklin**
6 **Ron Burgess**
7 **Stan Matthews**
8 **Kenny Dalglish**
9 **Tommy Lawton**
10 **Bobby Charlton**
11 **Billy Liddell**
Sub: Dave Mackay

'It was torture having to leave out so many great players, particularly so many masters from my own era. In the end I decided to go for a team that had the accent on attack. This would have been a dream team for spectators to watch.'

Tom Finney is the man many professionals pick as the *complete* player. He represented England in four different forward positions while winning 76 caps. Twice 'Footballer of the Year', he scored 187 goals for Preston in 431 appearances.

Brian Clough, tough, abrasive, successful

THE TEN CLUBS THAT HAVE HAD MOST POST-WAR MANAGERS*

1 Bury
Norman Bullock, John McNeil, Dave Russell, Bob Stokoe (2), Bert Head, Les Shannon, Jack Marshall, Les Hart, Colin McDonald, Tommy McAnearney, Allan Brown, Bobby Smith, Dave Hatton, Dave Connor, Jim Iley

2 Crewe Alexandra
George Lillycrop, Frank Hill, Arthur Turner, Harry Catterick, Ralph Ward, Maurice Lindley, Harry Ware, Jimmy McGuigan, Ernie Tagg (2), Dennis Viollet, Jimmy Melia, Harry Gregg, Warwick Rimmer, Tony Waddington, Arfon Griffiths

3 Crystal Palace
George Irwin, Jack Butler, Ronnie Rooke, Fred Dawes, Charlie Slade, Laurie Scott, Cyril Spiers, George Smith, Arthur Rowe, Dick Graham, Bert Head, Malcolm Allison (2), Terry Venables, Ernie Walley, Dario Gradi, Steve Kember, Alan Mullery

4 Darlington
Bill Forret, George Irwin, Bob Gurney, Dick Duckworth, Eddie Carr, Lol Morgan, Jimmy Greenhalgh, Ray Yeoman, Len Richley, Frank Brennan, Allan Jones, Ralph Brand, Dick Connor, Billy Horner, Peter Madden, Len Walker, Billy Elliott

5 Doncaster Rovers
Bill Marsden, Jack Bestall (2), Peter Doherty, Jack Hodgson, Syd Bycroft, Jack Crayston, Norman Curtis, Danny Malloy, Oscar Hold, Bill Leivers, Keith Kettleborough, George Raynor, Lawrie McMenemy, Maurice Setters, Stan Anderson, Billy Bremner

6 Grimsby Town
Charlie Spencer, Bill Shankly, Billy Walsh, Allenby Chilton, Tim Ward, Tom Johnston, Jimmy McGuigan, Don McEvoy, Bill Harvey, Bobby Kennedy, Lawrie McMenemy, Ron Ashman, Tommy Casey, John Newman, George Kerr, David Booth

7 Halifax Town
Jack Breedon, Len Wootton, Jimmy Thomson, Gerald Henry, Bobby Browne, Willie Watson (2), Billy Burnicle, Harry Hooper, Vic Metcalfe, Alan Ball snr. (2), George Kirby (2), Ray Henderson, George Mulhall, John Quinn, Jimmy Lawson, Mickey Bullock

8 Newport County
Billy McCandless, Tom Bromilow, Fred Stansfield, Bill Lucas (3), Bobby Evans, Trevor Morris, Les Graham, Bob Ferguson, Brian Harris, Dave Elliot, Jimmy Scoular, Colin Addison (2), Len Ashurst

9 Stockport County
Bob Marshall, Andy Beattie, Dick Duckworth, Willie Moir, Reg Flewin, Trevor Porteous, Bert Trautmann, Eddie Quigley (2), Jimmy Meadows (2), Walter Galbraith, Matt Woods, Brian Doyle, Roy Chapman, Alan Thompson, Mike Summerbee, Jimmy McGuigan, Eric Webster

10 Walsall
Harry Hibbs, Tony McPhee, Brough Fletcher, Major Buckley, John Love, Billy Moore (2), Alf Wood, Ray Shaw, Ron Lewin, Dick Graham, John Smith, Ronnie Allen, Doug Fraser, Dave Mackay, Alan Ashman, Frank Sibley, Alan Buckley (2), Neil Martin

(correct at time of going to press)

THE TEN CLUBS THAT HAVE HAD FEWEST POST-WAR MANAGERS

1 West Ham
Charlie Paynter, Ted Fenton, Ron Greenwood, John Lyall

2 Liverpool
George Kay, Don Welsh, Phil Taylor, Bill Shankly, Bob Paisley**

3 Southampton
Bill Dodgin (snr), Sid Cann, George Roughton, Ted Bates, Lawrie McMenemy

=4 Ipswich Town
Scott Duncan, Alf Ramsey, Jackie Milburn, Bill McGarry, Bobby Robson, Bobby Ferguson

Manchester United
Matt Busby (2), Wilf McGuinness, Frank O'Farrell, Tommy Docherty, Dave Sexton, Ron Atkinson

Spurs
Joe Hulme, Arthur Rowe, Jimmy Anderson, Bill Nicholson, Terry Neill, Keith Burkinshaw

=7 Arsenal
George Allison, Tom Whittaker, Jack Crayston, George Swindin, Billy Wright, Bertie Mee, Terry Neill

Barnsley
Angus Seed, Tim Ward, Johnny Steele, John McSeveney, Jim Iley, Allan Clarke, Norman Hunter

Nottingham Forest
Billy Walker, Andy Beattie, John Carey, Matt Gillies, Dave Mackay, Allan Brown, Brian Clough

Stoke City
Bob McGrory, Frank Taylor, Tony Waddington, George Eastham, Alan A'Court, Alan Durban, Richie Barker

**Joe Fagan was waiting in the wings to take over from the retiring Bob Paisley in the summer of 1983

LENNIE BENNETT'S DREAM TEAM

1 Bill Brown
2 Peter Baker
3 Ron Henry
4 Danny Blanchflower (capt)
5 Maurice Norman
6 Dave Mackay
7 Terry Medwin
8 John White
9 Bobby Smith
10 Les Allen
11 Cliff Jones
Sub: Terry Dyson

‘This is the Spurs team that won the League and FA Cup double in 1960–61 – a dream team if ever there was one. There wasn't a single weakness in the side and there has rarely been a team to match them for fluent football. And they were even better when Greavsie joined them the following season.’

Lennie Bennett, popular comedian and Punchlines presenter, is, would you believe, a Tottenham fanatic. He was a good-class footballer and started his working life as a sportswriter before switching to show business.

Dave Mackay, the 'Heart' of the Super Spurs side
and the 'Great Dictator' of Derby

TEN GREAT SCOTS WHO HAVE HAD THE BIGGEST INFLUENCE ON ENGLISH FOOTBALL

1 Matt Busby
2 Bill Shankly
3 Dave Mackay
4 Denis Law
5 Tommy Docherty
6 Kenny Dalglish
7 Billy Bremner
8 Bobby Collins
9 Frank McLintock
10 Billy Liddell

Jimmy Greaves: Sir Matt and Shanks were, of course, automatic choices because of their managerial triumphs after distinguished pre-war playing careers. I put Dave 'The Heart' Mackay ahead of my favourite Scot, Denis Law, because on top of his great playing achievements with Spurs and Derby he also lifted the League championship as Derby manager. There was no way I could leave out the ebullient Docherty, and Kenny Dalglish is high in my ratings simply because he is the finest player to come south in the last decade. Bremner, Collins and McLintock were all inspiring captains and Billy Liddell makes it just ahead of two other Liverpool idols, Ron Yeats and Graeme Souness. Jimmy Scoular was also on my short-list.

Derek Dougan (right), the saviour of Wolves

TEN IRISH IDOLS WHO HAVE HAD THE BIGGEST INFLUENCE ON ENGLISH FOOTBALL

1. **Danny Blanchflower**
2. **George Best**
3. **Derek Dougan**
4. **Terry Neill**
5. **Johnny Giles**
6. **Billy Bingham**
7. **Pat Jennings**
8. **Johnny Carey**
9. **Peter Doherty**
10. **Jimmy McIlroy**

Jimmy Greaves: Danny Blanchflower was the most influential player I ever played with or against. He was a real master of the arts and communicated his ideas to the players around him. Derek Dougan, the saviour of Wolves, and Terry Neill were both eloquent chairmen of the Professional Footballers' Association as well as being prominent players. George Best is high in my list simply because he was a genius.

TEN WELSH WONDERS WHO HAVE HAD THE BIGGEST INFLUENCE ON ENGLISH FOOTBALL

1 John Charles
2 Ron Burgess
3 Dave Bowen
4 Ivor Allchurch
5 Jack Kelsey
6 Cliff Jones
7 Mike England
8 Walley Barnes
9 John Toshack
10 Roy Vernon

Jimmy Greaves: John Charles is my No.1 choice even though he spent his peak years in Italy. He made sufficient impression at Leeds to prove that he was the greatest of all post-war Welsh footballers, with perhaps only Billy Meredith to challenge him in the all-time lists. Ron Burgess was considered by many good judges to have been Spurs' greatest ever player and Dave Bowen gets third place as much for steering Northampton to the First Division as his playing achievements with Arsenal. Roy Paul, Trevor Ford and Ron Davies were on my original short-list.

TONY JACKLIN'S DREAM TEAM

1 Pat Jennings
2 Bobby Moore (capt)
3 Roger Byrne
4 Duncan Edwards
5 Len Shackleton
6 Bobby Charlton
7 Stanley Matthews
8 Kevin Keegan
9 Tommy Lawton
10 Tom Finney
11 George Best
Sub: Frank Swift

'My dream team is revolutionary in that I have selected seven forwards. Once they get the ball, who's going to get it back off them, apart from when they have to pick it out of the net? A goalkeeper as substitute? I found it impossible to choose between Pat Jennings and Frank Swift, so they will play a half each.'

Tony Jacklin is one of Britain's greatest ever golfers. He won the British Open in 1969 and the US Open the following year. He remains the most popular British player on the world golf circuit.

THE TEN TOP CLUBS AND THEIR TOP TEAMS

The ten most successful Football League clubs since the war and a selection of their outstanding teams:

1 Liverpool
1965 FA Cup winners: Lawrence, Lawler, Byrne, Strong, Yeats, Stevenson, Callaghan, Hunt, St John, Smith, Thompson

European Cup winners 1977: Clemence, Neal, Jones, Smith, Kennedy, Hughes, Keegan, Case, Heighway, Callaghan, McDermott

1982–3 Championship squad: Grobbelaar, Neal, Kennedy, Thompson, Hansen, Lawrenson, Souness, Johnston, Lee, Whelan, Dalglish, Rush, Fairclough

2 Manchester United
1948 FA Cup winners: Crompton, Carey, Aston, Anderson, Chilton, Cockburn, Delaney, Morris, Rowley, Pearson, Mitten

1957 FA Cup squad: Wood, Foulkes, Byrne, Colman, Jackie Blanchflower, Edwards, Berry, Whelan, Taylor, Bobby Charlton, Viollett, Webster

1963 FA Cup winners: Gaskell, Dunne, Cantwell, Crerand, Foulkes, Setters, Giles, Quixall, Herd, Law, Bobby Charlton

1968 European Cup winners: Stepney, Brennan, Dunne, Crerand, Foulkes, Stiles, Best, Kidd, Bobby Charlton, Sadler, Aston

3 Spurs
1950–51 Push and Run League champions: Ditchburn, Ramsey, Willis (Withers), Nicholson, Clarke, Burgess, Walters, Bennett, Duquemin, Baily, Medley

1960–61 'Double' side: Brown, Baker, Henry, Danny Blanchflower, Norman, Mackay, Dyson (Medwin), White, Smith, Allen, Jones

1967 FA Cup winners: Jennings, Kinnear, Knowles, Mullery, England, Mackay, Robertson, Greaves, Gilzean, Venables, Saul. Sub: Jones

1981 FA Cup winners: Aleksic, Hughton, Miller, Roberts, Perryman, Villa, Ardiles, Archibald, Galvin, Hoddle, Crooks. Sub: Brooke

4 Wolves
1949 FA Cup winners: Williams, Pritchard, Springthorpe, Crook, Shorthouse, Wright, Hancock, Smyth, Pye, Dunn, Mullen

1960 FA Cup winners: Finlayson, Showell, Harris, Clamp, Slater, Flowers, Deeley, Stobart, Murray, Broadbent, Horne

1974 League Cup winners: Pierce, Palmer, Parkin, Bailey, Munro, McAlle, Sunderland, Hibbitt, Richards, Dougan, Wagstaffe. Sub: Powell

5 Arsenal
1950 FA Cup winners: Swindin, Scott, Barnes, Forbes, Leslie Compton, Mercer, Cox, Logie, Goring, Lewis, Denis Compton

1971–72 'Double' side: Wilson, Rice, McNab, Storey (Kelly), McLintock, Simpson, Armstrong, Graham, Radford, Kennedy, George

1979 FA Cup winners: Jennings, Rice, Nelson, Talbot, O'Leary, Young, Brady, Sunderland, Stapleton, Price, Rix. Sub: Walford

6 Leeds United
1965 FA Cup finalists: Sprake, Reaney, Bell, Bremner, Jackie Charlton, Hunter, Giles, Storrie, Peacock, Collins, Johanneson

1971 European Fairs Cup winners: Sprake, Reaney, Cooper, Bremner, Jackie Charlton, Hunter, Lorimer, Clarke, Jones, Giles, Madeley

7 Manchester City
1956 FA Cup winners: Trautmann, Leivers, Little, Barnes, Ewing, Paul, Johnstone, Hayes, Revie, Dyson, Clarke

1969 FA Cup winners: Dowd, Book, Pardoe, Doyle, Booth, Oakes, Summerbee, Bell, Lee, Young, Coleman

1981 FA Cup finalists: Corrigan, Ranson, McDonald, Reid, Power, Caton, Bennett, Gow, MacKenzie, Hutchison (Henry), Reeves (Tueart)

8 Nottingham Forest
1959 FA Cup winners: Thomson, Whare, McDonald, Whitefoot, McKinlay, Burkitt, Dwight, Quigley, Wilson, Gray, Imlach

1979 European Cup winners: Shilton, Anderson, Lloyd, Burns, Clark, Francis, McGovern, Bowyer, Robertson, Woodcock, Birtles

9 Newcastle United
1951 FA Cup winners: Simpson, Cowell, Corbett, Harvey, Brennan, Crowe, Walker, Taylor, Milburn, George Robledo, Mitchell

1955 FA Cup winners: Simpson, Cowell, Batty, Scoular, Stokoe, Casey, White, Milburn, Keeble, Hannah, Mitchell

1969 European Fairs Cup winners: McFaul, Craig, Clark, Gibb, Burton, Moncur, Scott, Robson, Davies, Arentoft, Sinclair

10 Everton=Aston Villa
Everton's 1966 FA Cup winners: West, Wright, Wilson, Gabriel, Labone, Harris, Scott, Trebilcock, Young, Harvey, Temple

Villa's 1957 FA Cup winners: Sims, Lynn, Aldis, Crowther, Dugdale, Saward, Smith, Sewell, Myerscough, Dixon, McParland

Villa's 1982 European Cup winners: Rimmer (Spink), Swain, Williams, Evans, McNaught, Mortimer, Bremner, Shaw, Withe, Cowans, Morley

THE TEN GREATEST BRITISH INTERNATIONAL TEAMS

1 England 1947
Swift, Scott, Hardwick, Wright, Franklin, Lowe, Matthews, Mortensen, Lawton, Mannion, Finney
Peak performance: Beat Portugal 10–0 in Lisbon in 1947

2 England 1961
Springett, Armfield, McNeil, Robson, Swan, Flowers, Douglas, Greaves, Smith, Haynes, Bobby Charlton
Peak performance: Beat Scotland 9–3 at Wembley in 1963

3 England 1966
Banks, Cohen, Wilson, Stiles, Jackie Charlton, Moore, Ball, Hunt, Bobby Charlton, Hurst, Peters
Peak peformance: 1966 World Cup victory *v.* West Germany

4 Scotland 1963
Bill Brown, Hamilton, Caldow, Mackay, Ure, Baxter, Henderson, White, St John, Law, Wilson
Peak performance: Beat England 2–1 at Wembley in 1963

5 Northern Ireland 1958
Uprichard, Keith, McMichael, Danny Blanchflower, Cunningham, Peacock, Bingham, Cush, Dougan, McIlroy, McParland
Peak performance: Beat Czechoslovakia 1–0 in 1958 World Cup

6 England 1969
Banks, Newton, Cooper, Mullery, Labone, Moore, Lee, Ball, Bobby Charlton, Hurst, Peters
Peak performance: Beat Scotland 4–1 at Wembley in 1969

7 Wales 1958
Kelsey, Stuart Williams, Hopkins, Sullivan, Mel Charles, Bowen, Medwin, Hewitt, John Charles, Ivor Allchurch, Cliff Jones
Peak performance: Beat Hungary 2–1 in 1958 World Cup

8 Scotland 1974
Harvey, Jardine, McGrain, Holton, Buchan, Bremner, Hay, Dalglish, Morgan, Jordan, Lorimer
Peak performance: 0–0 draw with Brazil in 1974 World Cup

9 England 1958
McDonald, Howe, Shaw, Clayton, Wright, Slater, Douglas, Bobby Charlton, Lofthouse, Haynes, Finney
Peak performance: Beat Russia 5–0 at Wembley in 1958

10 England 1981
Clemence, Neal, Mills, Thompson, Watson, Robson, Coppell, McDermott, Mariner, Brooking, Keegan. Sub: Wilkins
Peak performance: Beat Hungary 3–1 in Budapest in 1981

TEN GREAT PLAYERS WHO HAVE NOT GOT A SINGLE ENGLAND CAP TO SHOW AMONGST THEM*

1940s–1950s

1. **Jimmy Adamson**
2. **Ken Barnes**
3. **Jack Crompton**
4. **Jimmy Dugdale**
5. **Joe Harvey**
6. **Cliff Holton**
7. **Arthur Rowley**
8. **Bob Stokoe**
9. **Albert Stubbins**
10. **Charlie Wayman**

1960s–1980s

1. **George Armstrong**
2. **Billy Bonds**
3. **Tony Book**
4. **Jimmy Greenhoff**
5. **Ron Harris**
6. **Howard Kendall**
7. **Alan Oakes**
8. **Bryan 'Pop' Robson**
9. **Don Rogers**
10. **Maurice Setters**

Jimmy Adamson, one of the great uncapped players

ERIC MORECAMBE'S DREAM TEAM

1 Frank Swift
2 George Cohen
3 Ray Wilson
4 Nobby Stiles
5 George Young
6 Bobby Moore
7 Stanley Matthews
8 Ivor Broadis
9 Tom Finney
10 Duncan Edwards
11 George Best
Sub: Kenny Dalglish

'Come on folks. Be honest. What d'you think of it so far? I've always been in favour of fielding a *British* team against the world. You'd struggle to come up with a stronger combination. Even Luton would find it hard to beat them!'

Eric Morecambe, along with his side-kick Ernie Wise, has provided more pleasure for audiences these past forty-odd years than possibly any other British entertainer. He is Luton Town's No.1 fan and a former director.

TEN GREAT PLAYERS WHO EACH WON ONLY ONE INTERNATIONAL CAP*

1940s–1950s

1 **Ray Barlow**
2 **Geoff Bradford**
3 **Jimmy Hagan**
4 **Jimmy Logie**
5 **Willie Moir**
6 **Bill Nicholson**
7 **Jessie Pye**
8 **Stan Rickaby**
9 **Eddie Shimwell**
10 **Ernie Taylor**

1960s–1980s

1 **Tony Brown**
2 **Bill Foulkes**
3 **Charlie George**
4 **Colin Harvey**
5 **John Hollins**
6 **Phil Parkes**
7 **Steve Perryman**
8 **Ken Shellito**
9 **Alex Stepney**
10 **Tommy Smith**

THE TEN GREATEST POST-WAR FA CUP FINALS AT WEMBLEY

1 **Blackpool 4, Bolton Wanderers 3** (1953)
2 **Manchester United 4, Blackpool 2** (1948)
3 **Arsenal 3, Manchester United 2** (1979)
4 **Derby County 4, Charlton Athletic 1** (1946)
5 **Manchester United 3, Leicester City 1** (1963)
6 **Newcastle United 3, Manchester City 1** (1955)
7 **West Brom 3, Preston 2** (1954)
8 **Sunderland 1, Leeds United 0** (1974)
9 **Manchester City 3, Birmingham City 1** (1956)
10 **Wolves 3, Leicester City 1** (1949)

THE TEN GREATEST INDIVIDUAL PERFORMANCES IN POST-WAR FA CUP FINALS

1 **Stanley Matthews** (Blackpool *v.* Bolton 1953)
2 **Jackie Milburn** (Newcastle *v.* Blackpool, 1951)
3 **Nat Lofthouse** (Bolton *v.* Manchester United, 1958)
4 **Denis Law** (Manchester United *v.* Leicester City, 1963)
5 **Stan Mortensen** (Blackpool *v.* Bolton Wanderers, 1953)
6 **Peter McParland** (Aston Villa *v.* Man United, 1957)
7 **Joe Mercer** (Arsenal *v.* Newcastle United, 1952)
8 **Kevin Keegan** (Liverpool *v.* Newcastle United, 1974)
9 **Billy Wright** (Wolves *v.* Leicester City, 1949)
10 **Don Revie** (Manchester City *v.* Birmingham 1956)

TEN DEAD-EYE PENALTY TAKERS*

1 **Ronnie Allen (E)**
2 **Danny Blanchflower (NI)**
3 **Allan Clarke (E)**
4 **Ron Flowers (E)**
5 **Archie Gemmill (S)**
6 **Johnny Giles (Ei)**
7 **Kevin Keegan (E)**
8 **Phil Neal (E)**
9 **Alf Ramsey (E)**
10 **Terry Venables (E)**

GORDON BANKS'S DREAM TEAM

1 Pat Jennings
2 Jimmy Armfield
3 Ray Wilson
4 Duncan Edwards
5 John Charles (capt)
6 Dave Mackay
7 Tom Finney
8 John White
9 Alex Young
10 Bobby Charlton
11 George Best
Sub: Johnny Giles

‘I have gone for a team with the emphasis heavily on attack. You could switch these players to almost any formation and still have a formidable force capable of cracking any defence.’

Gordon Banks has many supporters as the greatest goalkeeper of all time. He was England's last line of defence in the team that won the 1966 World Cup and he kept a blank sheet in 35 of 73 international matches. England's full record when Gordon was in goal: P73 W49 D15 L9 F152 A57

TEN PLAYERS CURSED BY THE WEMBLEY INJURY JINX IN FA CUP FINALS

1952: **Walley Barnes**
Arsenal right-back *v.* Newcastle United. Torn knee ligaments

1953: **Eric Bell**
Bolton Wanderers left-half *v.* Blackpool. Pulled muscle

1955: **Jimmy Meadows**
Manchester City right-back *v.* Newcastle United. Wrenched knee

1956: **Bert Trautmann**
Manchester City goalkeeper *v.* Birmingham City. Broken neck

1957: **Ray Wood**
Manchester United goalkeeper *v.* Aston Villa. Fractured cheekbone

1959: **Roy Dwight**
Nottingham Forest right-winger *v.* Luton. Broken leg

1960: **Dave Whelan**
Blackburn Rovers right-back *v.* Wolves. Broken leg

1961: **Len Chalmers**
Leicester City right-back *v.* Spurs. Twisted knee

1972: **Mick Jones**
Leeds centre-forward *v.* Arsenal. Dislocated elbow

1978: **Liam Brady**
Arsenal midfield schemer *v.* Ipswich Town. Twisted ankle

TEN GREAT GOALS SCORED AT WEMBLEY*

Described by the men who scored them

1 Bobby Charlton *v.* Mexico, 1966 World Cup final
'I collected the ball just in our own half and set off on a run with the intention of eventually passing it to either Roger Hunt or Jimmy Greaves, who were both making diagonal runs ahead of me. The Mexican defenders scurried to cover Roger and Jimmy and a path opened for me down the middle. I was about thirty yards out in an inside-right position when I let fly with a right foot shot, and the ball crashed into the far corner of the net. It was particularly satisfying because it was England's first goal in the finals.'

2 Kevin Keegan for England *v.* Italy, 1977 World Cup qualifier
Trevor Brooking fired a beautifully flighted cross deep into the Italian penalty area. I raced towards the near post to meet it with my head and sent the ball wide of goalkeeper Dino Zoff and inside the far post. It was one of those moments when everything worked to perfection . . . the timing of my run, Trevor's pass, the weight and direction of my header. Everything.'

3 Rodney Marsh for QPR *v.* West Brom, 1967 League Cup final
We had been trailing 2–0 and had pulled back to 2–1 early in the second half. Then I collected the ball at about the halfway line and went off on a zig-zag run. I wrong-footed three West Brom defenders before steering a low right-foot shot into the net off a post from a few yards outside the box. We went on to win 3–2.'

4 Jackie Milburn for Newcastle United *v.* Blackpool, 1951 FA Cup final
Ernie Taylor back-heeled the ball into my path and I let fly with a first-time shot from the edge of the box. I knew from the moment the ball left my right boot it was going to be a goal. I

scored two goals in that match and the other one was just as satisfying. I side-footed the ball into the net from eighteen yards at the end of a long run with half the Blackpool defence snapping at my heels.’

5 Ferenc Puskas for Hungary *v.* England, 1953 international

‘It is a goal English people always talk about whenever I come to England. I was put through on the right-hand side of the England penalty area and sensed that Billy Wright was about to challenge me. I checked and dragged the ball back with the sole of my left boot and then, as Billy slid past me, shot with my left foot all in the same movement. The ball beat goalkeeper Gil Merrick at the near post. I was very proud of that moment because it was against a team I admired and on a ground that I had always wanted to play on.’

6 Len Shackleton for England *v.* West Germany, 1954 international

‘I noted that the German goalkeeper was very quick to come off his line to narrow the angle whenever a forward approached him. I made a mental note to try to lob him at the first opportunity. That's exactly what I did and it gave me great satisfaction to see him looking back helplessly as my calculated chip shot dropped over his head and into the net.’

7 Bobby Smith for Spurs *v.* Leicester City, 1961 FA Cup final

‘Terry Dyson pierced the Leicester defence with a neat through ball. I wrong-footed the Leicester defenders with a feint and then swivelled to beat Gordon Banks with a shot on the turn from fifteen yards.’

8 Dennis Tueart for Manchester City *v.* Newcastle United, 1976 League Cup final

‘Willie Donachie's long cross was knocked across goal by the head of Tommy Booth. The ball was going behind me and so I improvised with an overhead scissors kick that sent the ball thumping into the net from about eight yards.’

Bobby Smith, a Wembley goal-scoring hero for Spurs

9 Ricky Villa for Spurs *v.* Manchester City, 1981 FA Cup Final replay
Tony Galvin passed the ball inside to me from out on the left wing. I ran across the face of the Manchester City goal beating one, two and then three defenders. My idea was to pass the ball but then I saw a gap and so I shot low into the net with the goalkeeper sitting on his backside. It was a goal of a lifetime for me.'

10 Charlie Wayman for Preston v. West Brom, 1954 FA Cup final
The score was 1–1 when I was put clear just inside the West Brom half. All sorts of thoughts were rushing through my head as I raced nearly half the length of the pitch. I finally made up my mind to draw goalkeeper Jim Sanders. The thing I remember above all else is the deafening roar of the crowd as I fired the ball into the net at the end of a deperate chase. Unfortunately we lost the match 3–2 but I had the consolation of having scored in every round of the competition.'

BILLY BINGHAM'S DREAM TEAM

1 Frank Swift
2 Johnny Carey
3 Terry Cooper
4 Duncan Edwards
5 Mark Lawrenson
6 Martin Peters
7 George Best
8 Raich Carter
9 Tommy Lawton
10 Peter Doherty
11 Billy Liddell
Sub: Jimmy Greaves**

‘I gave careful consideration to the players of each decade in post-war football and found I was inclined to favour the Golden Oldies. This signifies that there were more great players around in the good old days. I've always been a Jimmy Greaves fan but can only find a place for him on the substitute's bench. I'm sure he would consider it an honour when he looks at the players who pipped him into my team.’

Billy Bingham, current Northern Ireland manager, was an outstanding winger with Sunderland, Luton and Everton. He steered Ireland to the 1982 World Cup finals, where they acquitted themselves exceptionally well, and he was a member of Northern Ireland's famous 1958 World Cup team.

**Editor's note: Guest selectors were specifically asked not to consider Jimmy Greaves for their teams.

TEN FAMOUS PLAYERS WHO MISSED TEN FAMOUS VICTORIES*

1 **Allan Brown**
(Blackpool v. Bolton Wanderers, 1953 FA Cup final; injured)

2 **Johnny Byrne**
(West Ham *v.* Munich 1860, 1965 European Cup Winners' Cup final; injured)

3 **Trevor Francis**
(Nottingham Forest *v.* SV Hamburg, 1980 European Cup final; injured)

4 **Jimmy Greaves****
(England *v.* West Germany, 1966 World Cup final; omitted)

5 **Alan Hudson**
(Chelsea *v.* Leeds United, 1970 FA Cup final; injured)

6 **Denis Law**
(Manchester United *v.* Benfica, 1968 European Cup final; injured)

7 **Dave Mackay**
(Spurs *v.* Atletico Madrid, 1963 European Cup Winners' Cup final; injured)

8 **Martin Peters**
(West Ham *v.* Preston, 1964 FA Cup final; omitted)

9 **Tommy Smith**
(Liverpool *v.* FC Bruges, 1978 European Cup final; injured)

10 **Mike Summerbee**
(Manchester City *v.* Gornik, 1970 European Cup Winners' Cup final; injured)

**Editor's selection

TEN WEMBLEY MATCHES THAT WENT TO EXTRA TIME

1 **Derby County *v* Charlton Athletic,** 1946 FA Cup final
2 **Charlton Athletic *v.* Burnley,** 1947 FA Cup final
3 **Liverpool *v.* Leeds United,** 1965 FA Cup final
4 **England *v.* West Germany,** 1966 World Cup final
5 **West Brom *v.* Everton,** 1968 FA Cup final
6 **Man United *v.* Benfica,** 1968 European Cup final
7 **Chelsea *v.* Leeds United,** 1970 FA Cup final
8 **Arsenal *v.* Liverpool,** 1971 FA Cup final
9 **Spurs *v.* Manchester City,** 1981 FA Cup final
10 **Spurs *v.* QPR,** 1982 FA Cup final

(League Cup finals not included)

WHAT THE FATHERS OF TEN FAMOUS FOOTBALLERS DID FOR A LIVING*

1 **Gordon Banks** (foundry worker, then bookmaker)
2 **George Best** (shipyard worker)
3 **Liam Brady** (docker)
4 **Trevor Brooking** (police inspector)
5 **Bobby Charlton** (coal miner)
6 **Allan Clarke** (long distance lorry driver)
7 **Jimmy Greaves** (tube train driver)
8 **Kevin Keegan** (coal miner)
9 **Denis Law** (trawlerman)
10 **Billy Wright** (iron founder)

TEN GREAT FA CUP GIANT KILLING ACTS

1 **Arsenal 0, Bradford 1** (1948)
2 **Arsenal 1, Norwich City 2** (1954)
3 **York City 2, Spurs 1** (1955)
4 **Derby County 1, Boston United 6** (1956)
5 **Wolves 0, Bournemouth 1** (1957)
6 **Norwich City 3, Manchester United 0** (1959)
7 **Chelsea 1, Crewe Alexandra 2** (1961)
8 **Peterborough 2, Arsenal 1** (1965)
9 **Colchester United 3, Leeds United 2** (1971)
10 **Hereford 2, Newcastle United 1** (1972)

TEN MORE GREAT FA CUP GIANT KILLING ACTS

1 **Yeovil 2, Sunderland 1** (1949)
2 **Everton 1, Leyton Orient 3** (1952)
3 **Port Vale 2, Blackpool (holders) 0** (1954)
4 **Bournemouth 3, Spurs 1** (1957)
5 **Tooting 3, Bournemouth 1** (1959)
6 **Worcester 2, Liverpool 1** (1959)
7 **Manchester City 1, Southampton 5** (1960)
8 **Oxford United 3, Blackburn Rovers 1** (1964)
9 **Newcastle United 1, Bedford Town 2** (1964)
10 **Stoke City 2, Blyth Spartans 3** (1978)

JOBS FOR THE BOYS*

What ten famous footballers did for a living before finding their feet in soccer

1 **Gordon Banks** (apprentice bricklayer)
2 **Garry Birtles** (tile layer)
3 **Tom Finney** (plumber's mate)
4 **Jack Kelsey** (blacksmith)
5 **Frank McLintock** (painter and decorator)
6 **Jackie Milburn** (pit engineer)
7 **Bill Nicholson** (laundry assistant)
8 **Frank Swift** (gasworks coke-keeper)
9 **Billy Wright** (tyre repairer)
10 **Ron Yeats** (apprentice slaughterman)

NEW CAREERS FOR OLD MASTERS*

What ten of England's 1966 World Cup squad are doing away from the game

1 **Jimmy Armfield** (sportswriter and broadcaster)
2 **Peter Bonetti** (runs a guest house on the Isle of Mull)
3 **Bobby Charlton** (partner in a travel agency)
4 **George Cohen** (land and property developer in Kent)
5 **John Connelly** (runs 'Connelly's Plaice', a fish and chip shop)
6 **Ron Flowers** (owns a sportsgoods shop in Wolverhampton)
7 **Roger Hunt** (director of a road haulage firm)
8 **Terry Paine** (mine host at the Prince of Wales, Cheltenham)
9 **Ron Springett** (owns a sportsgoods shop in Shepherds Bush)
10 **Ray Wilson** (a funeral director in West Yorkshire)

Jimmy Armfield (front), a master full-back who now writes about the game

TEN ENGLAND SCHOOLBOY INTERNATIONALS WHO BECAME FOOTBALL MASTERS*

1. **Raich Carter**
2. **Bobby Charlton**
3. **Duncan Edwards**
4. **Johnny Haynes**
5. **Stanley Matthews**
6. **Martin Peters**
7. **Len Shackleton**
8. **Peter Shilton**
9. **Nobby Stiles**
10. **Peter Thompson**

TEN FOOTBALL MASTERS WHO FAILED TO WIN ENGLAND SCHOOLBOY HONOURS*

1. **Jimmy Armfield**
2. **Alan Ball**
3. **Gordon Banks**
4. **Tom Finney**
5. **Jimmy Greaves****
6. **Roger Hunt**
7. **Kevin Keegan**
8. **Tommy Lawton**
9. **Bobby Moore**
10. **Billy Wright**

**Editor's selection

Raich Carter, a star even in his schooldays

BRENDAN FOSTER'S DREAM TEAM

1 Gordon Banks
2 Jimmy Armfield
3 Ray Wilson
4 Bryan Robson
5 Charlie Hurley
6 Duncan Edwards
7 Tom Finney
8 Kevin Keegan (capt)
9 Jackie Milburn
10 Bobby Charlton
11 Bobby Mitchell
Sub: Ossie Ardiles

‘I have naturally got a strong North-East flavour to my team and I've nominated Kevin Keegan as captain because of the way he has inspired every team he has ever played for. I know my team is supposed to be all-British, but I've slipped little Ossie Ardiles in on the sub's bench because he has been such a delight to watch since joining Spurs.’

Brendan Foster was one of Britain's greatest post-war middle-distance runners. He held world records at 3,000 metres and two miles, is the reigning Olympic 5,000 metres record holder and he won a procession of major titles. He is an enthusiastic Newcastle United supporter and currently joint managing director of Nike International and a respected member of the BBC–TV athletics commentary team.

BY DEGREES*

Ten famous footballers who had a university education

1 John Atyeo
2 Warren Bradley
3 Steve Coppell
4 Alan Gowling
5 Brian Hall
6 Steve Heighway
7 George Robb
8 Bill Slater
9 Tony Waiters
10 Bob Wilson

THE MASTER CLASS*

Former League players who have had schoolteaching experience

1 John Atyeo (E)
2 Warren Bradley (E)
3 Gil Merrick (E)
4 Arthur Milton (E)
5 George Robb (E)
6 Alex Tait (E)†
7 Allen Wade (E)†
8 Dennis Wilshaw (E)
9 Bob Wilson (S)
10 Phil Woosnam (W)

TEN GREAT ENGLAND PLAYERS WHO SCORED IN THEIR INTERNATIONAL DEBUTS*

1 **Bobby Charlton**
(*v.* Scotland 1958)

2 **Allan Clarke**
(penalty *v.* Czechoslovakia 1970 World Cup)

3 **Jimmy Greaves**
(*v.* Peru 1959)**

4 **Johnny Haynes**
(*v.* Northern Ireland 1955)

5 **Roger Hunt**
(*v.* Austria 1962)

6 **Nat Lofthouse**
(two goals *v.* Yugoslavia 1950)

7 **Wilf Mannion**
(three goals *v.* Northern Ireland 1946)

8 **Jackie Milburn**
(*v.* Northern Ireland 1948)

9 **Stan Mortensen**
(four goals *v.* Portugal 1947)

10 **Bobby Smith**
(*v.* Northern Ireland 1960)

**Editor's selection

Roger Hunt scored on his debut for England against Austria in 1962

TEN CONVERTED PLAYERS*

Footballers who went to rugby-playing schools

1 **Ronnie Allen (E)**
2 **Jimmy Armfield (E)**
3 **Ivor Broadis (E)**
4 **Alan Brown (E)†**
5 **Peter Downsborough (E)†**
6 **Steve Kindon (E)†**
7 **Joe Kirkup (E)†**
8 **Reg Matthews (E)**
9 **Malcolm Musgrove (E)†**
10 **Terry Yorath (W)**

THEY KNEW THE ROPES*

Ten footballers with boxing connections

1 **Ted Ditchburn (E)**
Son of pre-war professional boxer

2 **Wally Downes** (Wimbledon)
Nephew of former world middleweight champion, Terry Downes

3 **Justin Fashanu**
He was a promising amateur light-heavyweight boxer

4 **Mark Lazarus**
Brother of top-flight professionals, Lew and Harry Lazar

5 **Terry Mancini (E)**
From the famous boxing family (Len, Alf, Tony and Denny)

6 **Stanley Matthews (E)**
Son of a pre-war featherweight title contender

7 **Frank Morris** (Crystal Palace)
Won an ABA vest as a good-class amateur

8 **Dave Sexton**
His father, Archie, challenged for the British middleweight title

9 **Bill Shankly**
His dream was always to have been the world's middleweight champion

10 **Graham Shaw (E)**
He was a Great Britain schoolboy boxing champion

THE '200' CLUB

Ten players who have scored more than two hundred goals for one club in post-war football

315 John Atyeo (Bristol City)
255 Nat Lofthouse (Bolton Wanderers)
251 Arthur Rowley (Leicester City)
249 Roger Hunt (Liverpool)
245 Geoff Bradford (Bristol Rovers)
243 Gordon Turner (Luton Town)
220 Jimmy Greaves (Spurs)**
218 Tony Brown (West Brom)
204 Sammy Collins (Torquay United)
203 Ray Crawford (Ipswich Town)

**Editor's selection

TEN GREAT PLAYERS WHO NEVER WON A LEAGUE CHAMPIONSHIP MEDAL, OR PLAYED IN AN FA CUP FINAL*

1. **Ivor Allchurch**
2. **Jimmy Armfield**
3. **John Charles**
4. **Brian Clough**
5. **George Cohen**
6. **Johnny Haynes**
7. **Wilf Mannion**
8. **Martin Peters**
9. **Bobby Robson**
10. **Len Shackleton**

DENIS LAW'S DREAM TEAM

1 **Gordon Banks**
2 **Danny McGrain**
3 **Ray Wilson**
4 **Duncan Edwards**
5 **John Charles**
6 **Dave Mackay (capt)**
7 **George Best**
8 **Kenny Dalglish**
9 **Tom Finney**
10 **Jimmy Greaves**
11 **Bobby Charlton**
Sub: Johnny Haynes

‘In the unlikely event of this team being under pressure and maybe a goal down, big John Charles could switch to centre-forward. I'm ignoring instructions not to consider the great Jimmy Greaves for my dream team. It's unthinkable not to have the little feller in the attack. So there!’

Denis Law had a nickname in football that he always lived up to – The King. Nobody could match his penalty area reactions and the great Scot was an idol with both Manchester United and Manchester City. He is now a respected football analyst with Granada TV.

TEN GREAT PLAYERS WHO WERE NEVER VOTED FOOTBALLER OF THE YEAR*

The award was first introduced by the Football Writers' Association in 1947–48 when Stanley Matthews was elected 'Footballer of the Year'

1 **Alan Ball**
2 **Raich Carter**
3 **Johnny Giles**
4 **Johnny Haynes**
5 **Roger Hunt**
6 **Geoff Hurst**
7 **Denis Law**
8 **Tommy Lawton**
9 **Jackie Milburn**
10 **Len Shackleton**

TEN STAR PLAYERS WHO SLIPPED THROUGH THE NET*

Footballers who started their careers outside the Football League

1 **Garry Birtles** (Long Eaton)
2 **Tony Book** (Bath City)
3 **Alan Devonshire** (Southall)
4 **Steve Heighway** (Skelmersdale)
5 **Ian Hutchinson** (Cambridge United)
6 **Malcolm Macdonald** (Tonbridge)
7 **Cyrille Regis** (Hayes)
8 **Alex Stepney** (Tooting and Mitcham)
9 **Tony Waiters** (Macclesfield)
10 **Peter Ward** (Burton)

TEN STAR PLAYERS WHO WERE REJECTS*

1 **Phil Boyer (E)**
Rejected by Derby before starting his career with York City

2 **Ray Crawford (E)**
Portsmouth let him go to Ipswich Town after just eighteen games

3 **Tony Currie (E)**
He was turned down by QPR and Chelsea before joining Watford

4 **Kevin Keegan (E)**
Coventry gave him a trial but let him slip through their net to Scunthorpe

5 **Ray Kennedy (E)**
Port Vale let him go and Arsenal snapped him up

6 **Ted MacDougall (S)**
Rejected by Liverpool before starting his career with York City

7 **Mick Mills (E)**
Portsmouth had him as a youth player but released him and he joined Ipswich Town

8 **Jack Rowley (E)**
Started with Wolves who loaned him to Bournemouth without realizing his potential

9 **Ron Saunders (E)†**
Played just three games with Everton before going out of the League with Tonbridge

10 **Len Shackleton (E)**
He was on the Arsenal groundstaff but they let him go and he signed for Bradford

HAVE BOOTS WILL TRAVEL*

Ten centre-forwards who have had moving careers

1 **Wyn Davies**
Clubs: Wrexham, Bolton Wanderers, Newcastle United, Manchester City, Manchester United, Blackpool, Crystal Palace, Stockport County, Crewe Alexandra

2 **Jim Fryatt**
Clubs: Charlton Athletic, Southend, Bradford, Southport (2), Torquay (2), Stockport (2), Blackburn, Oldham

3 **Bobby Gould**
Clubs: Coventry, Arsenal, Wolves (2), West Brom, Bristol City, West Ham, Bristol Rovers, Hereford

4 **Tony Hateley**
Clubs: Notts County, Aston Villa, Chelsea, Liverpool, Coventry, Birmingham City, Notts County, Oldham

5 **Bob Hatton**
Clubs: Wolves, Bolton, Northampton, Carlisle, Birmingham City, Blackpool, Luton, Sheffield United, Cardiff City

6 **Cliff Holton**
Clubs: Oxford City, Arsenal, Watford (2), Northampton, Crystal Palace, Charlton Athletic, Leyton Orient

7 **Frank Large**
Clubs: Halifax, QPR, Northampton (3), Swindon, Carlisle, Oldham, Leicester City, Fulham, Chesterfield

8 **Ted MacDougall**
Clubs: Liverpool, York City, Bournemouth (2), Manchester United, West Ham, Norwich, Southampton, Blackpool

9 **Hugh McIlmoyle**
Clubs: Leicester City, Rotherham, Carlisle (3), Wolves, Bristol City, Middlesbrough, Preston

10 **John Manning**
Clubs: Tranmere (2), Shrewsbury, Norwich, Bolton, Walsall, Crewe Alexandra (2), Barnsley

FRANKIE VAUGHAN'S DREAM TEAM

1 Frank Swift
2 Alf Ramsey
3 Terry Cooper
4 Danny Blanchflower
5 Billy Wright (capt)
6 Duncan Edwards
7 Stanley Matthews
8 Jimmy Greaves
9 Bobby Charlton
10 Denis Law
11 George Best
Sub: Nobby Stiles

'I was born and raised a Liverpool supporter and had to torture myself to stop filling the team with Anfield favourites from when I was a youngster. Albert Stubbins and Billy Liddell were among a cluster of Golden Oldies who came easily to mind as I filled sheet after sheet with long short-lists! I finally arrived at this selection and I include Jimmy Greaves because I'm a crawler!'

Frankie Vaughan, 'Mr Personality' of show business who has been kicking around at the top for more than thirty years, was a good enough player to have made the grade as a professional footballer. But he succumbed to the moonlight and the girls!

Frank Swift, big safe hands, big warm heart

TEN SCANDALS THAT SHOOK THE SOCCER WORLD

1 Ten footballers were found guilty of conspiracy to defraud by 'fixing' matches and were all given prison sentences at Nottingham Assizes on 26 January 1965. They included England internationals Peter Swan and Tony Kay, and Sheffield Wednesday centre-forward David 'Bronco' Layne. The bribery scandal was uncovered by a team of *Sunday People* investigative reporters

2 Sunderland were found guilty of making illegal payments to players in 1957. The Sunderland chairman and three directors were suspended from football, the club was fined £5,000 and six players were ordered to forfeit their League benefit bonus

3 Port Vale were fined £4,000 and expelled from the League for making illegal payments to schoolboys and first-team players in 1968. The club were immediately re-elected to the Fourth Division

4 Peterborough were fined £500 and demoted from the Third to the Fourth Division in 1967 for making illegal payments to players

5 Derby County were fined £10,000 for alleged administrative irregularities in April 1970

6 Manchester United were fined £7,000 for alleged administrative irregularities in 1969

7 Tommy Docherty was sacked by Manchester United for alleged breach of contract just two months after leading the club to an FA Cup triumph at Wembley. He had decided to set up home with Mrs Mary Brown, the wife of the club physiotherapist. 'I have been punished for falling in love,' said The Doc

8 Bobby Moore was arrested in Bogota on the eve of the 1970 World Cup in Mexico and charged with stealing a bracelet from a jewellery shop. The England captain was released in time to play in the tournament and the charge was later dropped

9 Willie Johnston, West Brom winger, was found guilty of taking an illegal stimulant while playing for Scotland against Peru in the 1978 World Cup finals. He was immediately sent home and banned for a year by FIFA

10 The Irish League banned Coleraine inside-forward Johnny Crossan 'for life' in 1959 for receiving payment while an amateur. He played in Holland and Belgium until the ban was lifted in 1962, after which he played with distinction for Sunderland, Manchester City and Middlesbrough

TEN FAMOUS PEOPLE WHO WANTED TO BE FOOTBALLERS*

1 Ronnie Corbett
He was a schoolboy trialist with his local club, Hearts, for whom his cousin was a first-team player

2 David Essex
As David Cook, he was a schoolboy on West Ham's books and was in the same squad as Trevor Brooking

3 David Frost
He was an accomplished goalkeeper and Nottingham Forest were at one time interested in signing him

4 Elton John
Wanted to follow his uncle, Roy Dwight of Nottingham Forest, into professional football but stuck to the piano

5 Eddie Large
He was on Manchester City's books but his football dreams died at seventeen when he was knocked down by a bus

6 Des O'Connor
Northampton Town were interested in him but he chose instead to become a Butlin's Redcoat

7 Luciano Pavarotti
The world's No.1 opera star was an oustanding forward with Modena but chose singing ahead of soccer

8 Rod Stewart
He was an apprentice with Brentford with an ambition to score the winning goal for Scotland against England

9 Jimmy Tarbuck
Had two trials at Anfield before going full-time into show business. He is now one of Liverpool's No.1 fans

10 Mike Yarwood
He had a trial as a winger with Oldham and was told to go back when he had put on some more weight

TEN COMMANDMENTS FOR STRIKERS

1. Be first
2. Shoot on sight
3. Shoot straight
4. Stay close to the penalty box
5. Be selfish – you can't score without the ball
6. Suck up to the linesman – he can flag you to death
7. Ignore the coach yelling at you to 'tackle back'
8. Insult opposition defenders only if there's no return match later in the season
9. Never be nice to goalkeepers – they're enemy No.1
10. Celebrate your goals so that it registers that you scored. The next goal may be a long time off

TEN COMMANDMENTS FOR DEFENDERS

1 They shalt not pass
2 If in doubt, kick it out
3 Think before you tackle
4 As soon as the ball goes into your net look around for somebody to blame
5 Only be nasty on the blindside of the referee
6 Smile as you put the boot in – it won't look so bad
7 Never be nice to strikers – they're enemy No.1
8 Practise making the professional foul look like an accident
9 When the man you're marking scores, appeal for off-side, handball – *anything*
10 Never own up to an own goal

TEN COMMANDMENTS FOR MANAGERS

1 Always pick your *best* team
2 Earn the respect of your players
3 Convince your chairman you think he's the greatest
4 Get the ear of at least three influential media men
5 Refer to your players as 'us' in victory, 'them' in defeat
6 Keep supporters at arm's length (the longest possible arm)
7 Always wear a tracksuit when TV cameras are around
8 Be controversial (remember newspaper serialization fees)
9 Know when not to be in to the Press
10 Start job hunting when your chairman talks of his confidence in you

TEN COMMANDMENTS FOR REFEREES

1 Don't be seen wearing glasses or a deaf aid
2 Never be overruled by your linesman
3 Always befriend the captains – you may need them
4 If in doubt, give it to the home side
5 Think before you whistle
6 Never admit you're wrong
7 Always wear strong elastic in your shorts
8 Reconnoitre each ground for a back exit
9 If the TV cameras are there, smile and keep up with the play
10 Make sure there are no witnesses when you tell players and/or managers exactly what you think of them

TEN FOOTBALL CLICHÉS THAT SHOULD BE AVOIDED LIKE THE PLAGUE

1 Over the moon
2 Sick as a parrot
3 It's a funny game
4 You know, like
5 It was a game of two halves
6 Now we can concentrate on the League
7 The Cup's a great leveller
8 The mud's a great leveller
9 I'm well gutted
10 The game could have gone either way

TEN MOST USED EXCUSES IN DEFEAT

1 The ref' was diabolical
2 The pitch was diabolical
3 We didn't get the run of the ball
4 He was yards off-side
5 We should have had a penalty
6 The wind was against us
7 They kicked anything that moved
8 We've never had such a long injury list
9 The crowd didn't get behind us
10 They watered the bloody pitch

MY TEN FAVOURITE FOOT-BALL CLUB DIRECTORS

1
2
3
4
5
6
7
8
9
10

This list is an update on Len Shackleton's opinion of directors when he gave them a blank chapter in his autobiography back in the 1950s. Nothing's changed, Shack!

LEN SHACKLETON'S DREAM TEAM

1 Gordon Banks
2 Irving Nattrass
3 Kenny Sansom
4 Billy Bremner (capt)
5 Alan Hansen
6 Craig Johnston
7 Tom Finney
8 Peter Doherty
9 Brian Clough
10 Jimmy Greaves
11 George Best
Sub: Bobby Charlton

'In my first selection I had that marvellous Newcastle winger of the 1950s, Bobby Mitchell, in at outside-left but then I realized I just had to find a place for the Irish genius, George Best. So I reluctantly left Mitchell out. What a luxury to have a player of Bobby Charlton's calibre on the sub's bench! I've insisted on including Jimmy Greaves. He will make an ideal shooting partner for Brian Clough.'

Len Shackleton will always be remembered as the 'Clown Prince of Football' – one of the game's greatest entertainers as well as a superbly gifted inside-forward who could almost make a ball sit up and talk. He now entertains *Sunday People* readers with his North East soccer reports.

Archie Gemmill (right), thin on top but thick on talent

TEN GREAT PLAYERS THIN ON TOP BUT THICK ON TALENT*

1. **David Armstrong (E)**
2. **Ron Burgess (W)**
3. **Bobby Charlton (E)**
4. **Ralph Coates (E)**
5. **Archie Gemmill (S)**
6. **Alan Gilzean (S)**
7. **Terry Hennessey (W)**
8. **Andy Lochhead (S)†**
9. **Jimmy Melia (E)**
10. **Nobby Stiles (E)**

NICKNAMES THAT SUITED TEN GREAT PLAYERS*

1 **Nijinksy** (Colin Bell)
2 **The Gentle Giant** (John Charles)
3 **The Giraffe** (Jackie Charlton)
4 **Sniffer** (Allan Clarke)
5 **The Charmer** (Tommy Harmer)
6 **Crazy Horse** (Emlyn Hughes)
7 **Bites-Yer-Legs** (Norman Hunter)
8 **Wizard of Dribble** (Stanley Matthews)
9 **The Clown Prince** (Len Shackleton)
10 **The Ghost of White Hart Lane** (John White)

NICKNAMES THAT WOULD HAVE SUITED TEN GREAT PLAYERS*

1 **The Marathon Man** (George Armstrong)
2 **The Greatest** (George Best)
3 **Cinderella Man** (Tony Book)
4 **Anfield Assassin** (Kenny Dalglish)
5 **The Towering Inferno** (Micky Droy)
6 **Jaws III** (Joe Jordan)
7 **The Electric Heel** (Denis Law)
8 **The Headmaster** (Tommy Lawton)
9 **The Ice Berg** (Bobby Moore)
10 **The Incredible Bulk** (Bobby Smith)

John Charles, the Gentle Giant of football

MIKE YARWOOD'S DREAM TEAM

1 Pat Jennings
2 Alf Ramsey
3 Roger Byrne
4 Danny Blanchflower (capt)
5 Neil Franklin
6 Bobby Moore
7 Tom Finney
8 Trevor Francis
9 Kenny Dalglish
10 Denis Law
11 George Best
Sub: Duncan Edwards

> 'I could select at least six other teams equally as talented but I think this one would make a very good impression! I have made the great Duncan Edwards substitute simply because he could have filled any role in an emergency. Mr Greaves would have found a way into my attack, but I have left him out at his request.'

Mike Yarwood, the Voice of the Stars who is like a one man rent-a-crowd, wanted to go into football rather than show business. He had a trial as a teenage winger with Oldham Athletic and later became president of his home town club, Stockport County.

TEN SUPER SOCCER SALESMEN*

Football personalities who have been featured in nationwide advertising campaigns

1 **Gary Bailey** (Sharp electronics)
2 **Trevor Brooking** (Atari video games)
3 **Brian Clough** (Cadbury's chocolate buttons)
4 **Denis Compton** (Brylcreem)
5 **Tommy Docherty** (Gillette razors)
6 **Pat Jennings** (National Westminster Bank)
7 **Joe Jordan** (Heineken beer)
8 **Kevin Keegan** (Brut after-shave)
9 **Lawrie McMenemy** (Alcohol-free lager)
10 **Bobby Moore** (Bisto)

TEN PRODUCTS THEY COULD HAVE ADVERTISED*

1 **Malcolm Allison** (Dom Perignon champagne)
2 **George Best** (British Rail time-tables)
3 **John Bond** (Harmony hairspray)
4 **Bobby Charlton** (Crown toppers)
5 **Dave Mackay** (chest expanders)
6 **Rodney Marsh** (nutmeg powder)
7 **Stanley Matthews** (dummies for Mothercare)
8 **Bobby Moore** (jewellery)
9 **Nobby Stiles** (dentures)
10 **Terry Venables** (lawn mowers)

TEN REFEREES WHO WON RESPECT AS THEY WHISTLED WHILE THEY WORKED*

1 **Leo Callaghan**
2 **Ken Dagnall**
3 **Arthur Ellis**
4 **Jim Finney**
5 **Gordon Hill**
6 **Kevin Howley**
7 **Bob Matthewson**
8 **Pat Partridge**
9 **Jack Taylor**
10 **Clive Thomas**

Jimmy Greaves: Selecting the ten best referees is as personal a thing as picking a suit of clothes. These ten referees most suited my personal taste. Each of them showed a human side and was not a rule-book robot. They handled games with discretion and occasional humour that earned them the respect of the players.

Jack Taylor, always firm but fair

MIKE ENGLAND'S DREAM TEAM

1 Gordon Banks
2 Danny McGrain
3 Ray Wilson
4 Bobby Moore
5 John Charles
6 Duncan Edwards
7 Dave Mackay (capt)
8 Bobby Charlton
9 Tom Finney
10 Denis Law
11 George Best
Sub: Neil Franklin

‘I have selected my team in 4–3–3 formation, with Duncan Edwards, Dave Mackay and Bobby Charlton forming an unbeatable midfield trio. Where's the defence that could hope to stop the front three of Finney, Law and Best? The back four are all highly skilled as well as totally dependable under pressure, and Banksie at the back should not have a lot to do! I couldn't get Jimmy Greaves into my side but I'm sure he would love to work as the team's agent!’

Mike England, manager of the Welsh international team, was one of Britain's greatest centre-halves. He was capped forty-four times by Wales between 1962 and 1975 and was a master in the middle of the Blackburn and Spurs defences, despite recurring ankle injuries.

TEN PLAYERS WHO SWITCHED POSITIONS TO FIND FAME*

1 **Ronnie Allen (E)**
Started as an outside-right. Capped as a centre-forward

2 **Geoff Bradford (E)**
Started as a wing-half. Capped as a striker

3 **Roger Byrne (E)**
Started as an outside-left. Capped as a left-back

4 **Johnny Carey (Ei)**
Started as an inside-forward. Capped as a defender

5 **Terry Cooper (E)**
Started as an outside-left. Capped as a left-back

6 **Geoff Hurst (E)**
Started as a wing-half. Capped as a striker

7 **Jimmy Langley (E)**
Started as an outside-left. Capped as a left-back

8 **Malcolm MacDonald (E)**
Started as a left-back. Capped as a centre-forward

9 **Ron Pickering (E)**
Started as a full-back. Capped as a centre-forward

10 **Ray Wilson (E)**
Started as an outside-left. Capped as a left-back

MAX BYGRAVES'S DREAM TEAM

1 Diana Dors
2 Larry Grayson
3 Danny La Rue (capt)
4 Billy Wright
5 Beverley Sister I
6 Beverley Sister II
7 Beverley Sister III
8 Cyril Smith
9 John Bond
10 Mrs John Bond
11 Bo Derek
Sub: Blossom Bygraves

‘It probably wouldn't work as a team but it would certainly help the gate! When the team is on the attack everybody will come forward and Cyril Smith can drop back as a one-man defensive wall. Seriously though, *the* dream team has got to be England's 1966 World Cup winners.* They made so many dreams come true.’

*Gordon Banks, George Cohen, Ray Wilson, Nobby Stiles, Jackie Charlton, Bobby Moore (capt), Alan Ball, Roger Hunt, Bobby Charlton, Geoff Hurst, Martin Peters.

Max Bygraves, one of Britain's most popular entertainers, has always been a keen sports fan and at one time dreamed of becoming a professional boxing champion. As his team selection proves, few can match him for a sense of humour.

SECTION THREE

TEAM SELECTIONS

All players must have appeared for a Football League club in post-war matches.

ENGLAND SELECT

1940s–1950s

1 Frank Swift
2 Don Howe
3 Roger Byrne
4 Billy Wright (capt)
5 Neil Franklin
6 Duncan Edwards
7 Stanley Matthews
8 Raich Carter
9 Tommy Lawton
10 Johnny Haynes
11 Tom Finney
Sub: Wilf Mannion

1960s–1980s

1 Gordon Banks
2 Jimmy Armfield
3 Ray Wilson
4 Bryan Robson
5 Roy McFarland
6 Bobby Moore (capt)
7 Colin Bell
8 Roger Hunt
9 Bobby Smith
10 Bobby Charlton
11 Martin Peters
Sub: Nobby Stiles

SCOTLAND SELECT

1940s–1950s		*1960s–1980s*	
1	**Tommy Younger**	1	**Bob Wilson**
2	**Alex Parker**	2	**Tommy Gemmell**
3	**Willie Cunningham**	3	**Eddie McCreadie**
4	**Bobby Evans**	4	**Pat Crerand**
5	**Frank Brennan**	5	**Ron Yeats**
6	**Tommy Docherty (capt)**	6	**Dave Mackay (capt)**
7	**Bobby Collins**	7	**Jimmy Johnstone**
8	**Bobby Johnstone**	8	**Kenny Dalglish**
9	**Jackie Mudie**	9	**Denis Law**
10	**Billy Steel**	10	**Jim Baxter**
11	**Billy Liddell**	11	**John Robertson**
Sub:	**Jimmy Scoular**	**Sub:**	**Billy Bremner**

Above: Jim Baxter (left), all elegance and style for Scotland and Rangers
Left: Colin Bell (right), nicknamed Nijinsky by his Manchester City team-mates

WALES SELECT

1940s–1950s	*1960s–1980s*
1 Jack Kelsey	1 Gary Sprake
2 Walley Barnes	2 Peter Rodrigues
3 Alf Sherwood	3 Graham Williams
4 Dave Bowen	4 Terry Hennessey
5 John Charles	5 Mike England (capt)
6 Ron Burgess (capt)	6 Terry Yorath
7 Terry Medwin	7 Alan Durban
8 Roy Vernon	8 Ron Davies
9 Trevor Ford	9 Ian Rush
10 Ivor Allchurch	10 John Toshack
11 Cliff Jones	11 Leighton James
Sub: Roy Paul	Sub: Brian Flynn

NORTHERN IRELAND SELECT

1940s–1950s	*1960s–1980s*
1 Harry Gregg	1 Pat Jennings
2 Bob Keith	2 Pat Rice
3 Alf McMichael	3 Alex Elder
4 Danny Blanchflower (capt)	4 Martin Harvey
5 Jackie Blanchflower	5 Allan Hunter
6 Wilbur Cush	6 Terry Neill (capt)
7 Billy Bingham	7 Martin O'Neill
8 Peter Doherty	8 Norman Whiteside
9 Billy McAdams	9 Derek Dougan
10 Jimmy McIlroy	10 Sammy McIlroy
11 Peter McParland	11 George Best
Sub: Eddie McMorran	Sub: Gerry Armstrong

UNITED KINGDOM ALL-STARS

1940s–1950s

1 Frank Swift
2 Walley Barnes
3 Roger Byrne
4 Danny Blanchflower (capt)
5 John Charles
6 Duncan Edwards
7 Stanley Matthews
8 Raich Carter
9 Tommy Lawton
10 Jimmy McIlroy
11 Tom Finney
Sub: Billy Wright

1960s–1980s

1 Pat Jennings
2 Jimmy Armfield
3 Ray Wilson
4 Bobby Moore
5 Mike England
6 Dave Mackay (capt)
7 Kevin Keegan
8 Kenny Dalglish
9 Bobby Charlton
10 Denis Law
11 George Best
Sub: Bryan Robson

Stanley Matthews, the Wizard of Dribble

JASPER CARROTT'S DREAM TEAM

1 Gil Merrick
2 Jeff Hall
3 Gary Pendrey
4 Howard Kendall
5 Trevor Smith
6 Terry Hennessey (capt)
7 Gordon Astall
8 Frank Worthington
9 Eddy Brown
10 Trevor Francis
11 Archie Gemmill
Sub: Malcolm Page

'This is a very self-indulgent dream! They are just some of my favourite players who have featured with Birmingham City during the last thirty years. My team has a wonderful blend of speed and skill, plus of course total commitment. My apologies to that fine centre-forward, Bob Latchford, but Eddy Brown was my boyhood hero. Along with Len Shackleton, he was known as 'the Clown Prince of Football'. He used to shake hands with the corner flag and quote Shakespeare at opposition defenders. Oh, how we need him today!'

Jasper Carrott rose from terrace supporter to director of Birmingham City, the club with which he has had a love-hate relationship for thirty years. He is now more famous than the club as an entertainer with an acid wit.

ALL-STAR CLUB SELECTIONS

Author's Note: Wherever possible we have selected players for only one club – for instance, Mark Lawrenson for Brighton but not for Liverpool.

Arsenal select

1 Jack Kelsey (W)
2 Walley Barnes (W)
3 Ken Sansom (E)
4 David O'Leary (Ei)
5 Frank McLintock (S)
6 Joe Mercer (E) (capt)
7 George Armstrong (E)
8 Charlie George (E)
9 Frank Stapleton (Ei)
10 Liam Brady (Ei)
11 Tony Woodcock (E)
Sub: Ray Kennedy (E)

Aston Villa select

1 Jimmy Rimmer (E)
2 Kenny Swain (E)†
3 John Gidman (E)
4 Allan Evans (S)
5 Ken McNaught (S)†
6 Dennis Mortimer (E)† (capt)
7 Des Bremner (S)
8 Andy Gray (S)
9 Peter Withe (E)
10 Gordon Cowans (E)
11 Peter McParland (NI)
Sub: Vic Crowe (W)

Birmingham City select

1 Gil Merrick (E)
2 Jeff Hall (E)
3 Colin Green (W)
4 Terry Hennessey (W) (capt)
5 Trevor Smith (E)
6 Malcolm Page (W)
7 Gordon Astall (E)
8 Trevor Francis (E)
9 Bob Latchford (E)
10 Bertie Auld (S)
11 Mike Hellawell (E)
Sub: Ken Leek (W)

Blackburn select

1 Harry Leyland (E)†
2 Keith Newton (E)
3 Bill Eckersley (E)
4 Ron Clayton (E)
5 Mike England (W)
6 Barry Hole (W)
7 Bryan Douglas (E)
8 Peter Dobing (E)†
9 Derek Dougan (NI)
10 Roy Vernon (W)
11 Bobby Langton (E)
Sub: Andy McEvoy (Ei)

Blackpool select

1 George Farm (S)
2 Jimmy Armfield (E) (capt)
3 Eddie Shimwell (E)
4 Ernie Taylor (E)
5 Harry Johnston (E)
6 Emlyn Hughes (E)
7 Stanley Matthews (E)
8 Stan Mortensen (E)
9 Jackie Mudie (S)
10 Allan Brown (S)
11 Bill Perry (E)
Sub: Ray Charnley (E)

Bolton Wanderers select

1 Eddie Hopkinson (E)
2 Roy Hartle (E)†
3 Tommy Banks (E)
4 John Wheeler (E)
5 John Higgins (E)†
6 Bryan Edwards (E)†
7 Francis Lee (E)
8 Freddie Hill (E)
9 Nat Lofthouse (E) (capt)
10 Ray Parry (E)
11 Harold Hassall (E)
Sub: Malcolm Barrass (E)

Brighton select

1 Graham Moseley (E)†
2 Sammy Nelson (NI)
3 Mel Hopkins (W)
4 Jimmy Case (E)†
5 Steve Foster (E) (capt)
6 Mark Lawrenson (Ei)
7 Neil McNab (S)†
8 Mick Robinson (Ei)
9 Bobby Smith (E)
10 Peter Ward (E)
11 Andy Ritchie (E)†
Sub: Gordon Smith (S)†

Burnley select

1 Colin McDonald (E)
2 John Angus (E)
3 Alex Elder (NI)
4 Martin Dobson (E)
5 Tommy Cummings (E)†
6 Jimmy Adamson (E)† (capt)
7 Willie Morgan (S)
8 Ralph Coates (E)
9 Ray Pointer (E)
10 Jimmy McIlroy (NI)
11 John Connelly (E)
Sub: Leighton James (W)

Chelsea select

1 **Peter Bonetti (E)**
2 **Ken Shellito (E)**
3 **Eddie McCreadie (S)**
4 **John Hollins (E)**
5 **John Dempsey (Ei)**
6 **Ron Harris (E)† (capt)**
7 **Alan Hudson (E)**
8 **Peter Osgood (E)**
9 **Roy Bentley (E)**
10 **Charlie Cooke (S)**
11 **Bobby Tambling (E)**
Sub: Frank Blunstone (E)

Coventry City select

1 **Reg Matthews (E)**
2 **Danny Thomas (E)**
3 **Terry Yorath (W) (capt)**
4 **Gerry Daly (Ei)**
5 **Jeff Blockley (E)**
6 **Gerry Francis (E)**
7 **Tommy Hutchison (S)**
8 **Willie Carr (S)**
9 **Colin Stein (S)**
10 **Ian Wallace (S)**
11 **Ronnie Rees (W)**
Sub: George Curtis (E)†

Crystal Palace select

1 **John Jackson (E)†**
2 **Paddy Mulligan (Ei)**
3 **Kenny Sansom (E)**
4 **Jim Cannon (S)†**
5 **John Sewell (capt) (E)†**
6 **Peter Wall (E)†**
7 **Don Rogers (E)†**
8 **George Graham (S)**
9 **Johnny Byrne (E)**
10 **Steve Kember (E)†**
11 **Peter Taylor (E)**
Sub: Vince Hilaire (E)†

Terry Yorath, a driving force in midfield

Derby County select

1 Vic Woodley (E)
2 Rod Thomas (W)
3 Jack Howe (E)
4 Alan Durban (W)
5 Roy McFarland (E) (capt)
6 Colin Todd (E)
7 Kevin Hector (E)
8 Raich Carter (E)
9 John O'Hare (S)
10 Peter Doherty (NI)
11 Alan Hinton (E)
Sub: Bruce Rioch (S)

Everton select

1 Gordon West (E)
2 Tommy Wright (E)
3 Ray Wilson (E)
4 Jimmy Gabriel (S)
5 Brian Labone (E) (capt)
6 Colin Harvey (E)
7 Bobby Collins (E)
8 Alan Ball (E)
9 Alex Young (S)
10 Joe Royle (E)
11 Derek Temple (E)
Sub: Fred Pickering (E)

Fulham select

1 Tony Macedo (E)†
2 George Cohen (E)
3 Jim Langley (E)
4 Alan Mullery (E)
5 Jim Taylor (E)
6 Eddie Lowe (E)
7 Graham Leggatt (S)
8 Bobby Robson (E)
9 Bedford Jezzard (E)
10 Johnny Haynes (E) (capt)
11 Rodney Marsh (E)
Sub: Jimmy Hill (E)†

Ipswich Town select

1 Roy Bailey (E)†
2 George Burley (S)
3 Mick Mills (E) (capt)
4 Arnold Muhren (H)
5 Allan Hunter (NI)
6 Kevin Beattie (E)
7 Frans Thijssen (H)
8 Paul Mariner (E)
9 Ray Crawford (E)
10 Ted Phillips (E)†
11 Jimmy Leadbetter (S)†
Sub: John Wark (S)

Leeds United select

1 **Gary Sprake (W)**
2 **Paul Reaney (E)**
3 **Terry Cooper (E)**
4 **Billy Bremner (S) (capt)**
5 **Jackie Charlton (E)**
6 **Norman Hunter (E)**
7 **Peter Lorimer (S)**
8 **Allan Clarke (E)**
9 **John Charles (W)**
10 **Johnny Giles (Ei)**
11 **Eddie Gray (S)**
Sub: Paul Madeley (E)

Johnny Giles (left), a pass master for Leeds and Eire

Leicester City select

1 **Mark Wallington (E)†**
2 **Steve Whitworth (E)**
3 **Willie Bell (S)**
4 **Colin Appleton (E)†**
5 **Ian King (S)†**
6 **David Nish (E) (capt)**
7 **Keith Weller (E)**
8 **Arthur Rowley (E)†**
9 **Frank Worthington (E)**
10 **Davie Gibson (S)**
11 **Mike Stringfellow (E)†**
Sub: Graham Cross (E)†

Liverpool select

1 **Ray Clemence (E)**
2 **Chris Lawler (E)**
3 **Gerry Byrne (E)**
4 **Phil Thompson (E)**
5 **Ron Yeats (S) (capt)**
6 **Tommy Smith (E)**
7 **Kevin Keegan (E)**
8 **Roger Hunt (E)**
9 **Ian St John (S)**
10 **Kenny Dalglish (S)**
11 **Billy Liddell (S)**
Sub: Ian Callaghan (E)

Luton Town select

1 **Ron Baynham (E)**
2 **Brendan McNally (Ei)**
3 **Bobby Thomson (E)**
4 **Bob Morton (E)†**
5 **Syd Owen (E) (capt)**
6 **Bruce Rioch (S)**
7 **Billy Bingham (NI)**
8 **Gordon Turner (E)†**
9 **Malcolm Macdonald (E)**
10 **Paul Walsh (E)**
11 **Brian Stein (E)†**
Sub: George Cummins (Ei)

Manchester City select

1 **Frank Swift (E)**
2 **Tony Book (E)†**
3 **Willie Donachie (S)**
4 **Mike Doyle (E)**
5 **Tommy Booth (E)†**
6 **Roy Paul (W) (capt)**
7 **Mike Summerbee (E)**
8 **Colin Bell (E)**
9 **Don Revie (E)**
10 **Bobby Johnstone (S)**
11 **Peter Barnes (E)**
Sub: Alan Oakes (E)†

COLIN COWDREY'S DREAM TEAM

1 Gordon Banks
2 Alf Ramsey
3 Roger Byrne
4 Billy Wright (capt)
5 Neil Franklin
6 Duncan Edwards
7 Stanley Matthews
8 Stan Mortensen
9 Tommy Lawton
10 Bobby Charlton
11 Tom Finney
Sub: Bobby Moore

'I would like to have got one or two Charlton Athletic players into the team, but in the end I went for the best man for each position. To have a player of Bobby Moore's calibre on the substitute's bench is an indication of the all-round strength of the team.'

Colin Cowdrey played in a record 114 Tests for England and 23 of this master batsman's 107 centuries came in Test matches. He has been a director of Charlton Athletic, the club always closest to his heart.

Manchester United select

1 **Alex Stepney (E)**
2 **John Carey (Ei)**
3 **Roger Byrne (E) (capt)**
4 **Pat Crerand (S)**
5 **Martin Buchan (S)**
6 **Duncan Edwards (E)**
7 **Bryan Robson (E)**
8 **Denis Law (S)**
9 **Tommy Taylor (E)**
10 **Bobby Charlton (E)**
11 **George Best (NI)**
Sub: Nobby Stiles (E)

Middlesbrough select

1 **Jim Platt (NI)**
2 **Mick McNeil (E)**
3 **George Hardwick (E) (capt)**
4 **Bill Harris (W)**
5 **Mel Nurse (W)**
6 **Eric McMordie (NI)**
7 **Graeme Souness (S)**
8 **Wilf Mannion (E)**
9 **Brian Clough (E)**
10 **Alan Peacock (E)**
11 **Eddie Holliday (E)**
Sub: Craig Johnston (SA)†

Newcastle United select

1 **Ronnie Simpson (S)**
2 **Bobby Moncur (S)**
3 **Alf McMichael (NI)**
4 **Joe Harvey (E)† (capt)**
5 **Frank Brennan (S)**
6 **Jimmy Scoular (S)**
7 **Terry McDermott (E)**
8 **Malcolm Macdonald (E)**
9 **Jackie Milburn (E)**
10 **Ivor Allchurch (W)**
11 **Bobby Mitchell (S)**
Sub: Bryan Robson (E)†

Norwich City select

1 **Kevin Keelan (E)†**
2 **Ron Ashman (E)† (capt)**
3 **Ollie Burton (W)**
4 **Martin O'Neill (NI)**
5 **Duncan Forbes (S)†**
6 **Martin Peters (E)**
7 **Kevin Reeves (E)**
8 **Ron Davies (W)**
9 **Terry Bly (E)†**
10 **Ted MacDougall (S)**
11 **Phil Boyer (E)**
Sub: Ralph Hunt (E)†

Nottingham Forest select

1 Peter Shilton (E)
2 Viv Anderson (E)
3 Frank Gray (S)
4 John McGovern (S)† (capt)
5 Larry Lloyd (E)
6 Martin O'Neill (NI)
7 Ian Storey-Moore (E)
8 Kenny Burns (S)
9 Garry Birtles (E)
10 Archie Gemmill (S)
11 John Robertson (S)
Sub: Bob McKinlay (S)†

Notts County Select

1 Radojko Avramovic (Yug)
2 Tristan Benjamin (WI)†
3 Ray O'Brien (Ei)
4 Leon Leuty (E)†
5 Brian Kilkline (E)†
6 Don Masson (S)
7 Frank Broome (E)
8 Jeff Astle (E)
9 Tommy Lawton (E) (capt)
10 Tony Hateley (E)†
11 Jackie Sewell (E)
Sub: Les Bradd (E)†

Portsmouth select

1 Ernie Butler (E)†
2 Jimmy Stephen (S)
3 Harry Ferrier (E)†
4 Jimmy Scoular (S) (capt)
5 Reg Flewin (E)†
6 Jimmy Dickinson (E)
7 Peter Harris (E)
8 Duggie Reid (E)†
9 Ike Clarke (E)†
10 Len Phillips (E)
11 Jack Froggatt (E)
Sub: Johnny Gordon (E)†

Preston select

1 Alan Kelly (Ei)
2 Willie Cunningham (S)
3 Jim Smith (S)†
4 Tommy Docherty (S) (capt)
5 Frank O'Farrell (Ei)
6 Howard Kendall (E)†
7 Peter Thompson (E)
8 Charlie Wayman (E)†
9 Tom Finney (E)
10 Alex Dawson (S)†
11 Doug Holden (E)
Sub: Willie Irvine (NI)

QPR Select

1 **Ron Springett (E)**
2 **Dave Clement (E)**
3 **Ian Gillard (E)**
4 **Ivor Powell (W)**
5 **Frank McLintock (S) (capt)**
6 **Gerry Francis (E)**
7 **Terry Venables (E)**
8 **Stan Bowles (E)**
9 **Les Allen (E)†**
10 **Rodney Marsh (E)**
11 **Tony Currie (E)**
Sub: Brian Bedford (E)†

Sheffield United Select

1 **Alan Hodgkinson (E)**
2 **Len Badger (E)†**
3 **Graham Shaw (E)**
4 **Alex Forbes (S)**
5 **Joe Shaw (E)† (capt)**
6 **Trevor Hockey (W)**
7 **Alan Woodward (E)†**
8 **Jimmy Hagan (E)**
9 **Mick Jones (E)**
10 **Tony Currie (E)**
11 **Colin Grainger (E)**
Sub: Gil Reece (W)

Tony Currie (right), a dream schemer for Queen's Park Rangers

Sheffield Wednesday select

1 **Ron Springett (E)**
2 **Wilf Smith (E)† (capt)**
3 **Don Megson (E)†**
4 **Tony Kay (E)**
5 **Peter Swan (E)**
6 **Gerry Young (E)**
7 **Albert Quixall (E)**
8 **Jackie Sewell (E)**
9 **Derek Dooley (E)†**
10 **Redfern Froggatt (E)**
11 **John Fantham (E)**
Sub: Terry Curran (E)†

Southampton select

1 **Peter Shilton (E)**
2 **Peter Rodrigues (W) (capt)**
3 **Stuart Williams (W)**
4 **Jim Steele (S)†**
5 **Dave Watson (E)**
6 **Jim McCalliog (S)**
7 **Terry Paine (E)**
8 **Mike Channon (E)**
9 **Martin Chivers (E)**
10 **Ron Davies (W)**
11 **David Armstrong (E)**
Sub: Phil Boyer (E)

Stoke City select

1 **Gordon Banks (E)**
2 **John Marsh (E)†**
3 **Mike Pejic (E)**
4 **John Mahoney (W)**
5 **Neil Franklin (E) (capt)**
6 **Sammy McIlroy (NI)**
7 **Mark Chamberlain (E)**
8 **Roy Vernon (W)**
9 **John Ritchie (E)†**
10 **Dennis Viollett (E)**
11 **George Eastham (E)**
Sub: Jimmy Greenhoff (E)†

Sunderland select

1 **Jim Montgomery (E)†**
2 **Dick Malone (S)†**
3 **Martin Harvey (NI)**
4 **Stan Anderson (E)**
5 **Charlie Hurley (Ei) (capt)**
6 **Jim Baxter (S)**
7 **Billy Bingham (NI)**
8 **Len Shackleton (E)**
9 **Trevor Ford (W)**
10 **Tony Towers (E)**
11 **Dennis Tueart (E)**
Sub: Ray Daniel (W)

Swansea City select

1 Dai Davies (W)
2 Nigel Stevenson (W)
3 Herbie Williams (W)
4 Roy Paul (W) (capt)
5 Mel Nurse (W)
6 Mel Charles (W)
7 Terry Medwin (W)
8 Bob Latchford (E)
9 Trevor Ford (W)
10 Ivor Allchurch (W)
11 Cliff Jones (W)
Sub: Len Allchurch (W)

Tottenham select

1 Pat Jennings (NI)
2 Alf Ramsey (E)
3 Ron Burgess (W)
4 Danny Blanchflower (NI) (capt)
5 Maurice Norman (E)
6 Dave Mackay (S)
7 Eddie Baily (E)
8 John White (S)
9 Bobby Smith (E)
10 Glenn Hoddle (E)
11 Osvaldo Ardiles (Arg)
Sub: Steve Perryman (E)

Watford select

1 Pat Jennings (NI)
2 Pat Rice (NI) (capt)
3 John Williams (E)†
4 Duncan Welbourne (E)†
5 Steve Sims (E)†
6 Tom Walley (W)
7 Billy Jennings (E)†
8 Luther Blissett (E)
9 Cliff Holton (E)†
10 Gerry Armstrong (NI)
11 John Barnes (E)†
Sub: Ross Jenkins (E)†

West Brom select

1 John Osborne (E)†
2 Don Howe (E) (capt)
3 Graham Williams (W)
4 Tony Brown (E)
5 John Wile (E)†
6 John Kaye (E)†
7 Willie Johnston (S)
8 Cyrille Regis (E)
9 Ronnie Allen (E)
10 Jeff Astle (E)
11 Asa Hartford (S)
Sub: Bobby Hope (S)

West Ham United select		*Wolves select*	
1	**Phil Parkes (E)**	1	**Bert Williams (E)**
2	**Frank Lampard (E)**	2	**Mike Bailey (E)**
3	**Noel Cantwell (Ei)**	3	**Bobby Thomson (E)**
4	**Billy Bonds (E)†**	4	**Ron Flowers (E)**
5	**Alvin Martin (E)**	5	**Billy Wright (E) (capt)**
6	**Bobby Moore (E) (capt)**	6	**Bill Slater (E)**
7	**Peter Brabrook (E)**	7	**Johnny Hancocks (E)**
8	**Geoff Hurst (E)**	8	**Dennis Wilshaw (E)**
9	**Johnny Byrne (E)**	9	**Jesse Pye (E)**
10	**Trevor Brooking (E)**	10	**Peter Broadbent (E)**
11	**Martin Peters (E)**	11	**Jimmy Mullen (E)**
Sub:	**Alan Devonshire (E)**	**Sub:**	**John Richards (E)**

Geoff Hurst completes his historic 1966 World Cup hat-trick

GREAT FOOTBALLING FAMILIES

Two teams of well-matched brothers

1 Peter Springett (E)†
2 Bernard Shaw (E)†
3 Bryn Jones (W)†
4 Danny Blanchflower (NI) (capt)
5 Jackie Charlton (E)
6 John Hollins (E)
7 Eddie Gray (S)
8 Jack Rowley (E)
9 John Charles (W)
10 Ivor Allchurch (W)
11 Roger Morgan (E)†
Sub: Bobby Irvine (NI)

1 Ron Springett (E)
2 Graham Shaw (E)
3 Frank Gray (S)
4 Ian Morgan (E)†
5 Jackie Blanchflower (NI)
6 Mel Charles (W)
7 Len Allchurch (W)
8 Arthur Rowley (E)†
9 Willie Irvine (NI)
10 Bobby Charlton (E) (capt)
11 Cliff Jones (W)
Sub: Dave Hollins (W)

Fathers v. Sons

1 Roy Bailey (E)†
2 John Bond (E)†
3 Alan Ball snr (E)†
4 Tommy Docherty (S) (capt)
5 Ken Barnes (E)†
6 Mel Charles (W)
7 Les Allen (E)†
8 Jimmy Greaves (E)**
9 Tony Hateley (E)†
10 Alec Herd (S)
11 George Eastham snr (E)
Sub: Ivor Jones (W)

1 Gary Bailey (E)†
2 Kevin Bond (E)†
3 Alan Ball jnr (E) (capt)
4 Michael Docherty (E)†
5 Peter Barnes (E)
6 Jeremy Charles (W)
7 Clive Allen (E)†
8 Danny Greaves (E)**
9 Mark Hateley (E)†
10 David Herd (S)
11 George Eastham jnr (E)
Sub: Bryn Jones (W)†

**Editor's selection

LORD 'TED' WILLIS'S DREAM TEAM

1 Peter Shilton
2 Alf Ramsey
3 Alan Kennedy
4 Danny Blanchflower (capt)
5 Leslie Compton
6 Dave Mackay
7 Cliff Jones
8 Kenny Dalglish
9 Bobby Smith
10 John White
11 George Best
Sub: Graeme Souness

'I wish to make the point that James Greaves Esquire would have been an automatic choice but for the fact that you gave him a red card! I have not included overseas players, otherwise I would have found a place for Ossie Ardiles. And, oh how I wish we had a central defender today who was half as good as Leslie Compton. He was a magnificent man in the middle for Arsenal in the immediate post-war years and it was shameful that he had to wait until he was thirty-eight for his first England cap. He and his brother Denis gave football as well as cricket wonderful service.'

Lord Willis, creator of 'Dixon of Dock Green' and a distinguished writer, has been a life-long Spurs fan.

ALL-STAR STAR-SIGN TEAMS

Capricorn
(21 Dec–19 Jan)
(4–4–2)

Gordon Banks (E)
30.12.37
Steve Perryman (E)
21.12.51
John Charles (W)
27.12.31
Frank McLintock (S) (capt)
28.12.39
Mick Mills (E)
4.1.49
Bryan Robson (E)
11.1.57
Raich Carter
21.12.13
Johnny Giles (Ei)
6.1.40
Eddie Gray (S)
17.1.48
Malcolm Macdonald (E)
7.1.50
Billy Liddell (S)
10.1.22
Sub:
Stan Bowles (E)
24.12.48

Aquarius
(20 Jan–18 Feb)
(4–2–4)

Bert Williams (E)
31.1.20
Alf Ramsey (E)
22.1.20
Billy Wright (E)
6.2.24
Neil Franklin (E)
24.1.22
Roger Byrne (E)
8.2.29
Danny Blanchflower (NI) (capt)
20.2.26
Liam Brady (Ei)
13.2.56
Stanley Matthews (E)
1.2.15
Kevin Keegan (E)
14.2.51
Tommy Taylor (E)
29.1.32
Cliff Jones (W)
7.2.35
Sub:
Bobby Robson (E)
18.2.33

Pisces

(19 Feb–20 Mar)
(3–4–3)

Lawrie Leslie (S)
17.3.35
Pat Rice (NI)
17.3.49
Martin Buchan (S)
6.3.49
Johnny Carey (Ei) (capt)
23.2.19
Mike Bailey (E)
27.2.42
Colin Bell (E)
26.2.46
Kenny Dalglish (S)
4.3.51
Jimmy Greaves (E)**
20.2.40
Peter Osgood (E)
20.2.47
Bobby Smith (E)
22.2.33
Denis Law (S)
24.2.40
Sub:
Trevor Cherry (E)
23.2.48

**Editor's selection

Aries

(21 Mar–20 Apl)
(4–2–4)

Gary Sprake (W)
3.4.45
Ken Shellito (E)
18.4.40
Roy McFarland (E)
5.4.48
Bobby Moore (E) (capt)
12.4.41
Eddie McCreadie (S)
15.5.40
Tommy Smith (E)
5.4.45
Ian Callaghan (E)
10.4.42
Terry Paine (E)
23.3.39
Brian Clough (E)
21.3.35
John Toshack (W)
22.3.49
Tom Finney (E)
5.4.22
Sub:
Terry Yorath (W)
27.3.50

Taurus

(21 Apl–20 May)
(3–4–3)

Gordon West (E)
24.4.43
Laurie Scott (E)
23.4.17
Jackie Charlton (E)
8.5.35
David O'Leary (Ei)
2.5.58
Nobby Stiles (E)
18.5.42
Alan Ball (E) (capt)
12.5.45
Len Shackleton (E)
3.5.22
Wilf Mannion (E)
16.5.18
Graeme Souness (S)
6.5.53
Jackie Milburn (E)
11.5.24
Francis Lee (E)
29.4.44
Sub:
Jimmy Dickinson (E)
24.4.25

Gemini

(21 May–21 Jne)
(4–2–4)

Pat Jennings (NI)
12.6.45
George Burley (S)
3.6.56
Alan Hansen (S) (capt)
13.6.55
Mark Lawrenson (Ei)
2.6.57
David Craig (NI)
8.6.54
Bryan Douglas (E)
27.5.42
Alan Brazil (S)
15.6.59
Graham Leggatt (S)
20.6.34
Stan Mortensen (E)
26.5.42
Ron Davies (W)
25.4.42
George Best (NI)
22.5.46
Sub:
Peter Barnes (E)
10.6.57

Nobby Stiles, the Toothless Tiger

Cancer

(21 Jne–21 Jly)
(4–4–2)

George Farm (S)
13.7.24
Keith Newton (E)
23.6.41
Allan Hunter (NI)
30.6.46
Cyril Knowles (E)
13.7.44
Terry Cooper (E)
12.7.44
John Hollins (E)
16.7.46
Don Revie (E) (capt)
10.7.27
Alan Durban (W)
7.7.41
Alan Hudson (E)
21.6.51
Roger Hunt (E)
20.7.38
Willie Wallace (S)
23.6.42
Sub:
Bill Eckersley (E)
16.7.26

Leo

(22 Jly–21 Aug)
(3–4–3)

Ray Clemence (E)
5.8.48
Alex Parker (S)
2.8.35
Ron Flowers (E)
28.7.34
Joe Mercer (E) (capt)
9.8.14
Ossie Ardiles (Arg)
3.8.52
Eddie Baily (E)
6.8.25
John Wark (S)
4.8.57
Sammy McIlroy (NI)
2.8.54
Albert Quixall (E)
9.8.33
Allan Clarke (E)
31.7.46
Bobby Murdoch (S)
17.8.44
Sub:
Ronnie Clayton (E)
5.8.34

Virgo
(22 Aug–21 Sept)
(4–4–2)

Peter Shilton (E)
18.9.49
Jimmy Armfield (E) (capt)
21.9.35
Leslie Compton (E)
12.9.12
Paul Madeley (E)
20.9.44
Emlyn Hughes (E)
28.8.47
Barry Hole (W)
16.9.42
Ray Wilkins (E)
14.9.56
Terry Hennessey (W)
1.9.42
Ernie Taylor (E)
2.9.25
Nat Lofthouse (E)
27.8.25
Bobby Tambling (E)
18.9.41
Sub:
Tony Book (E)†
4.9.35

Libra
(22 Sept–22 Oct)
(4–4–2)

Bert Trautmann (Ger)
22.10.23
George Cohen (E)
22.10.39
Dave Watson (E)
5.10.46
Kenny Burns (S)
23.9.53
Kenny Sansom (E)
26.9.58
Ivor Allchurch (W)
16.10.29
Johnny Haynes (E) (capt)
17.10.34
Jim Baxter (S)
29.9.39
Duncan Edwards (E)
1.10.36
Tommy Lawton (E)
6.10.19
Bobby Charlton (E)
11.10.37
Sub:
George Eastham (E)
23.9.36

Scorpio
(23 Oct–21 Nov)
(4–3–3)

Ted Ditchburn (E)
24.10.21
Mel Hopkins (W)
7.11.34
Ron Yeats (S)
15.11.37
Dave Mackay (S) (capt)
14.11.34
Frank Gray (S)
27.10.54
Glenn Hoddle (E)
27.10.57
Martin Peters (E)
8.11.43
Norman Hunter (E)
29.10.43
Bryan 'Pop' Robson (E)†
11.11.45
Kevin Hector (E)
2.11.44
Mark Chamberlain (E)
19.11.61
Sub:
Brian Flynn (W)
12.10.55

Sagittarius
(22 Nov–20 Dec)
(4–2–4)

Jack Kelsey (W)
19.11.29
Colin Todd (E)
12.12.48
Mike England (W)
2.12.41
Kevin Beattie (E)
18.12.53
Ray Wilson (E)
17.12.34
Alan Mullery (E)
23.11.41
Billy Bremner (S) (capt)
9.12.42
Peter Lorimer (S)
14.12.46
Mike Channon (E)
28.11.48
Geoff Hurst (E)
8.12.41
Frank Worthington (E)
23.11.48
Sub:
Terry McDermott (E)
8.12.51

Peter Lorimer, football's hottest shot

ROY HUDD'S DREAM TEAM

1 John Jackson
2 Alfie Noakes (capt)
3 Peter Wall
4 Terry Venables
5 John Sewell
6 Paddy Mulligan
7 Don Rogers
8 Alan Whittle
9 Rachid Harkouk
10 Charlie Cooke
11 Peter Taylor
Sub: Johnny 'Budgie' Byrne

'This would be not so much a dream as a nightmare! They are all Crystal Palace players who have brought me more frustration, laughs and pure pleasure than any other players I have ever seen. And I love them all.'

As Roy Hudd's selection just might indicate, he is a dedicated follower of Crystal Palace. Roy has been in show business for more than twenty years and is an acknowledged expert on the history of the music-hall. He has become one of England's best-loved funnymen.

A TEAM OF COCKNEYS

Players born in the Greater London area

1 **Peter Bonetti** (Putney)
2 **George Cohen** (Kensington)
3 **Ken Sansom** (Camberwell)
4 **Alan Mullery** (Notting Hill)
5 **David O'Leary** (Stoke Newington)
6 **Bobby Moore** (Barking) (capt)
7 **Peter Brabrook** (East Ham)
8 **Jimmy Greaves** (East Ham)**
9 **Malcolm Macdonald** (Fulham)
10 **Johnny Haynes** (Edmonton)
11 **Martin Peters** (Plaistow)
Sub: Trevor Brooking (Barking)

**Editor's selection

A TEAM OF SCOUSERS

Players born in Liverpool

1 Andy Rankin†
2 Tommy Wright
3 Phil Thompson
4 Roy McFarland
5 Brian Labone (capt)
6 Tommy Smith
7 Steve Coppell
8 Peter Withe
9 Joe Royle
10 Joe Baker
11 Ian Callaghan
Sub: Jimmy Melia

A TEAM OF GLASWEGIANS

Players born in Glasgow

1 Ron Simpson
2 Tommy Gemmell
3 Eddie McCreadie
4 Tommy Docherty
5 Frank McLintock (capt)
6 Jim Baxter
7 Jimmy Johnstone
8 Kenny Dalglish
9 Andy Gray
10 Bobby Collins
11 Eddie Gray
Sub: Willie Morgan

A TEAM OF MANCUNIANS

Players born in Manchester

1 Joe Corrigan
2 Keith Newton
3 Roger Byrne (capt)
4 Nobby Stiles
5 Harry Johnston
6 Mike Doyle
7 Peter Barnes
8 Tony Towers
9 Brian Kidd
10 Stan Bowles
11 Doug Holden
Sub: Wilf McGuinness

A TEAM OF BELFAST BHOYOS

Players born in Belfast

1 Hugh Kelly
2 Pat Rice
3 Alf McMichael
4 Danny Blanchflower (capt)
5 Terry Neill
6 Jimmy Nicholson
7 Billy Bingham
8 Gerry Armstrong
9 Derek Dougan
10 Sammy McIlroy
11 George Best
Sub: Martin Harvey

A TEAM OF DUBLINERS

Players born in Dublin

1 Alan Kelly
2 Tony Dunne
3 John Carey (capt)
4 Mick Martin
5 Mick McGrath
6 Liam Brady
7 Joe Haverty
8 Con Martin
9 Frank Stapleton
10 Johnny Giles
11 Steve Heighway
Sub: Paddy Mulligan

A TEAM OF GEORDIES

Players born in the North-East

1 **Ray Wood** (Hebburn)
2 **Derek Parkin** (Newcastle)
3 **Colin Todd** (Chester-le-Street)
4 **Bobby Robson** (Langley Park)
5 **Jackie Charlton** (Ashington)
6 **Bryan Robson** (Chester-le-Street)
7 **Colin Bell** (Heselden)
8 **Raich Carter** (Sunderland)
9 **Jackie Milburn** (Ashington)
10 **Bobby Charlton** (Ashington) (capt)
11 **Jimmy Mullen** (Newcastle)
Sub: Ray Kennedy (Seaton Delavel)

A TEAM OF LANCASTRIANS

Players born in Lancashire

1 **Frank Swift** (Blackpool)
2 **Jimmy Armfield** (Blackpool) (capt)
3 **Emlyn Hughes** (Barrow)
4 **Ronnie Clayton** (Preston)
5 **Bill Slater** (Clitheroe)
6 **Alan Ball** (Farnworth)
7 **Bryan Douglas** (Blackburn)
8 **Nat Lofthouse** (Bolton)
9 **Tommy Lawton** (Bolton)
10 **Roger Hunt** (Golborne)
11 **Tom Finney** (Preston)
Sub: Geoff Hurst (Ashton)

A TEAM OF MIDLANDERS

Players born in the Midlands

1 **Peter Shilton** (Leicester)
2 **Don Howe** (Wolverhampton)
3 **David Nish** (Burton)
4 **Billy Wright** (Ironbridge) (capt)
5 **Dave Watson** (Stapleford)
6 **Duncan Edwards** (Dudley)
7 **Stanley Matthews** (Hanley)
8 **Allan Clarke** (Willenhall)
9 **Bob Latchford** (Birmingham)
10 **Jack Rowley** (Wolverhampton)
11 **Tony Woodcock** (Nottingham)
Sub: Neil Franklin (Stoke)

Jackie Milburn, the idol of Tyneside

Gordon Banks, safe as the Banks of England

A TEAM OF YORKSHIREMEN

Players born in Yorkshire

1 **Gordon Banks** (Sheffield)
2 **Paul Madeley** (Leeds)
3 **Ray Wilson** (Shirebrook)
4 **Tony Kay** (Sheffield)
5 **Peter Swan** (South Elmsall)
6 **Norman Hunter** (Eighton Banks)
7 **Albert Quixall** (Sheffield)
8 **Wilf Mannion** (South Bank)
9 **Tommy Taylor** (Barnsley)
10 **Len Shackleton** (Bradford)
11 **Kevin Keegan** (Doncaster) (capt)
Sub: Terry Cooper (Castleford)

A TEAM OF SWANS

Players born in Swansea

1 **Jack Kelsey**
2 **John Roberts**
3 **Barry Hole**
4 **Mel Nurse**
5 **Ray Daniel**
6 **Mel Charles**
7 **Terry Medwin**
8 **Trevor Ford**
9 **John Charles (capt)**
10 **Ivor Allchurch**
11 **Cliff Jones**
Sub: Barrie Jones

A TEAM OF WEST COUNTRYMEN

Players born in the West Country

1 **Roger Jones** (Upton)†
2 **Peter Sillett** (Southampton)
3 **Bill Ellerington** (Southampton)
4 **Maurice Setters** (Honiton)†
5 **Larry Lloyd** (Bristol)
6 **Trevor Francis** (Plymouth)
7 **Terry Paine** (Winchester)
8 **Mike Channon** (Orcheston)
9 **Roy Bentley** (Bristol) (capt)
10 **Martin Chivers** (Southampton)
11 **John Atyeo** (Westbury)
Sub: Geoff Bradford (Bristol)

A TEAM OF FOREIGN-BORN PLAYERS

(Country of origin in brackets)

1 **Bert Trautmann** (Germany)
2 **Ivan Golac** (Yugoslavia)
3 **John Hewie** (South Africa)
4 **Arnold Muhren** (Holland)
5 **Terry Butcher** (Singapore)
6 **Craig Johnston** (South Africa)
7 **Allan Simonsen** (Denmark)
8 **Osvaldo Ardiles** (Argentine)
9 **Cyrille Regis** (French Guyana)
10 **George Robledo** (Chile)
11 **Bill Perry** (South Africa)
Sub: Eddie Firmani (South Africa)

A TEAM OF GREAT PLAYERS WHO WERE FORCED OUT OF FOOTBALL BY INJURY

1 **Colin McDonald (E)**
Debut 1953. Retired 1958 aged 28

2 **Ken Shellito (E)**
Debut 1958. Retired 1965 aged 25

3 **John Lyall (E)†**
Debut 1959. Retired 1962 aged 22

4 **Jimmy Meadows (E)**
Debut 1948. Retired 1954 aged 23

5 **Wilf McGuinness (E)**
Debut 1955. Retired 1959 aged 22

6 **Tony Green (S)**
Debut 1966. Retired 1972 aged 26

7 **Brian Little (E)**
Debut 1971. Retired 1979 aged 26

8 **Brian Clough (E)**
Debut 1955. Retired 1964 aged 28

9 **Derek Dooley (E)**
Debut 1946. Retired 1953 aged 22

10 **Ian Hutchinson (E)†**
Debut 1968. Retired 1974 aged 26

11 **Ian Storey-Moore (E)**
Debut 1963. Retired 1973 aged 28

Sub: Alick Jeffrey (E)†
Debut 1954. Retired 1969 aged 29

JIMMY YOUNG'S DREAM TEAM

1 Frank Moss
2 George Male
3 Eddie Hapgood
4 Jack Crayston
5 Herbie Roberts
6 Wilf Copping
7 Joe Hulme
8 David Jack
9 Ted Drake
10 Alex James
11 Cliff Bastin
Sub: Stanley Matthews

‘I know I've broken the rules by dipping into the pre-war period for my dream team, but this Arsenal side of the 1930s was just unbeatable. They won just about everything except the Boat Race. Stanley Matthews as substitute? Well, he guested for the Gunners in that famous match against Moscow Dynamo. Imagine the feelings of the opposition left-back facing the speed and thrust of Joe Hulme and knowing that ‘Wizard of Dribble’ Matthews was waiting, so to speak, in the wings!’

Jimmy Young, big band singer-turned-DJ-turned-radio-interviewer, is – as you might have guessed – an Arsenal fan. He reminds us of the traditions of Arsenal with the unforgettable team that first lured him to Highbury.

A TEAM OF ENGLAND CAPTAINS

(The number of times they have led England in brackets)

1 Frank Swift (2)
2 Jimmy Armfield (15)
3 George Hardwick (13)
4 Emlyn Hughes (23)
5 Billy Wright (90) (capt)
6 Bobby Moore (90)
7 Alan Ball (6)
8 Kevin Keegan (31)
9 Bobby Charlton (3)
10 Johnny Haynes (22)
11 Martin Peters (3)
Sub: Ronnie Clayton (5)

Bobby Moore gets carried away as England's 1966 World Cup captain

A TEAM OF BLACK DIAMONDS

Black players who have made an impressive impact in the Football League (4–2–4 formation)

1 **Alex Williams** (Manchester City)
2 **Viv Anderson** (Nottingham Forest)
3 **Chris Whyte** (Arsenal)
4 **Bob Hazell** (QPR)
5 **Brendon Batson** (West Brom)
6 **Remi Moses** (Manchester United)
7 **Danny Thomas** (Coventry City)
8 **Mark Chamberlain** (Stoke City)
9 **Cyrille Regis** (West Brom)
10 **Luther Blissett** (Watford)
11 **Garth Crooks** (Spurs)
Sub: Clyde Best (West Ham)

STRIKERS UNITED

A team of goalscorers with their total League goals in brackets

1 Alex Stepney (2)
2 Phil Neal (62)
3 David Nish (39)
4 Bobby Robson (133)
5 John Charles (173)
6 Ray Kennedy (118)
7 Tom Finney (187)
8 Jimmy Greaves (357)**
9 Nat Lofthouse (255)
10 John Atyeo (315)
11 Bobby Charlton (206)
Sub: Roger Hunt (269)

**Editor's selection

Jimmy Greaves, on a familiar route to goal**
**Editor's selection

BY THE LEFT

A team of international players who have been left-footed artists

1 Ray Clemence (E)
2 Eddie McCreadie (S)
3 Ray Wilson (E)
4 Ray Kennedy (E)
5 Roy McFarland (E) (capt)
6 Norman Hunter (E)
7 Eddie Gray (S)
8 George Eastham (E)
9 Derek Dougan (NI)
10 Liam Brady (Ei)
11 Alan Hinton (E)
Sub: John Dick (S)

A TEAM OF GREAT UNCAPPED PLAYERS

1 Sam Bartram
2 Tony Book
3 Ron Harris
4 Billy Bonds (capt)
5 Joe Harvey
6 Jimmy Adamson
7 George Armstrong
8 Arthur Rowley
9 Cliff Holton
10 Bryan 'Pop' Robson
11 Don Rogers
Sub: Howard Kendall

DAVID FROST'S DREAM TEAM

1 John Burke
2 Charlie Marks
3 George Dorling
4 Jimmy Boswell
5 Tom Kingsnorth
6 Gilbert Piper
7 Johnny Warsap
8 'Willie' Wilson
9 Hugh Russell
10 Johnny Briggs
11 George Forrester

‘Gillingham was the team I supported as a youngster and this was the side that earned us re-election to the Football League back in 1950. This eleven-year-old was over the moon!’

David Frost, the best-known British television presenter in the world, has always been a football 'freak' who never misses the opportunity to show off his goalkeeping ability in charity matches. He could have made it as a professional with Nottingham Forest but 'That Was the Week That Was' beckoned and he has been in orbit as a superstar ever since.

A WELL-SCHOOLED TEAM

England internationals who had a grammar school education

1 **Tony Waiters** (King George V Grammar, Southport)
2 **Jimmy Armfield** (Arnold Grammar, Blackpool)
3 **Roger Byrne** (Burnage Grammar, Manchester) (capt)
4 **Johnny Haynes** (Latymer Grammar, Edmonton)
5 **Bill Slater** (Clitheroe Grammar, Manchester)
6 **Colin Harvey** (Cardinal Allen Grammar, Liverpool)
7 **Alan Ball** (Farnworth Grammar, Lancs)
8 **Roger Hunt** (Leigh Grammar, Lancs)
9 **Malcolm Macdonald** (Sloane Grammar, Tonbridge)
10 **John Atyeo** (Trowbridge High, Wilts)
11 **Bobby Charlton** (Bealington Grammar, Ashington)
Sub: Keith Newton (Didsbury Grammar, Manchester)

OVER THE BAR

A team of internationals who have held publican's licences

1 Peter Bonetti (E)
2 Eddie Shimwell (E)
3 Tony Allen (E)
4 Frank McLintock (S)
5 John Charles (W)
6 Bobby Moore (E) (capt)
7 Terry Paine (E)
8 Martin Chivers (E)
9 Peter Osgood (E)
10 Jim Baxter (S)
11 Jimmy Johnstone (S)
Sub: John Radford (E)

OWZAT! FOOTBALLING CRICKETERS

1 **Jim Cumbes** (Worcestershire, Lancashire & Surrey)
West Brom & Aston Villa goalkeeper
2 **Ken Taylor** (Yorkshire & England)
Huddersfield & Bradford Park Avenue
3 **Cyril Poole** (Nottinghamshire & England)
Mansfield Town
4 **Willie Watson** (Yorkshire, Leicestershire & England)
Huddersfield, Sunderland & England
5 **Leslie Compton** (Middlesex)
Arsenal & England
6 **Brian Close** (Yorkshire, Somerset & England)
Leeds United
7 **Arthur Milton** (Gloucestershire & England)
Arsenal, Bristol City & England
8 **Chris Balderstone** (Yorkshire, Leicestershire & England)
Huddersfield, Doncaster & Carlisle
9 **Ian Botham** (Somerset & England)
Scunthorpe reserves, plus two substitute appearances in League
10 **Graham Cross** (Leicestershire)
Leicester City, Chesterfield, Brighton, Preston & Lincoln
11 **Denis Compton** (Middlesex & England)
Arsenal and England war-time international
Sub: Jim Standen (Worcestershire)
Arsenal, Luton Town, West Ham, Millwall & Portsmouth goalkeeper

THE BUSINESSMAN'S SPECIAL

A team of former Football League players who became successful businessmen

1 **Malcolm Finlayson**
Managing director of a Midlands steel firm

2 **George Cohen**
Land and property developer in Kent

3 **Tommy Banks**
A building contractor in Bolton

4 **George Hardwick**
Chairman of a structual steel firm in Saltburn

5 **Ron Flowers**
Owner of a sports goods business in Wolverhampton

6 **Abe Rosenthal**
A leading ice-cream manufacturer

7 **Francis Lee**
Managing Director of a large wastepaper recycling business

8 **Roger Hunt**
Director of a road haulage business in Lancashire

9 **Jesse Pye**
A hotelier in Blackpool

10 **Albert Quixall**
Scrap metal merchant

11 **Tom Finney**
Head of a plumbing and electrical business in Preston

Sub: David Whelan
Boss of a supermarket chain in Lancashire

George Cohen, always dependable right-back for Fulham and England

A TEAM TO BREAK THE BANK

A squad of the most expensive players in the land

1 **Phil Parkes (E)**
£565,000, from QPR to West Ham. World record for a goalkeeper

2 **John Gidman (E)**
£600,000, Aston Villa to Everton. British record for a right-back

3 **Kenny Sansom (E)**
£1,350,000, Crystal Palace to Arsenal. Record for a full-back

4 **Bryan Robson (E)**
£1,500,000, West Brom to Manchester United. British record

5 **Mark Lawrenson (Ei)**
£900,000, Brighton to Liverpool

6 **Steve Daley (E)†**
£1,437,500, Norwich City to Manchester City

7 **Ian Wallace (S)**
£1,250,000, Coventy City to Nottingham Forest

8 **Trevor Francis (E)**
£1,200,000, Nottingham Forest to Manchester City

9 **Andy Gray (S)**
£1,469,000, Aston Villa to Wolves

10 **Frank Stapleton (Ei)**
£1,100,000, Arsenal to Manchester United

11 **Garry Birtles (E)**
£1,250,000, Nottingham Forest to Manchester United

Sub: Clive Allen (E)†
£1,250,000, Crystal Palace to Arsenal

Jimmy Greaves: The total cost of this team is a staggering £13,871,500. All the deals took place between 1979 and 1981 when clubs were crazily chucking money around like confetti. Kevin Reeves and Justin Fashanu are the only million-pound players not included in the squad. Manchester City, Manchester United and Nottingham Forest have each paid three £1m transfer fees. Clive Allen and Trevor Francis have each been involved in two £1m transfers.

Garry Birtles (right) cost Manchester United a cool £1¼ million

A WORLD CUP TELLY TEAM

A team of ex-footballers who appeared on TV during the 1982 World Cup finals

1 Bob Wilson (BBC)
2 John Bond (ITV)
3 Ron Atkinson (ITV)
4 Billy Wright (ITV) (capt)
5 Jackie Charlton (ITV)
6 Jimmy Hill (BBC)
7 Denis Law (ITV)
8 Brian Clough (ITV)
9 Ian St John (ITV)
10 Bobby Charlton (BBC)
11 George Best (ITV)
Sub: Jimmy Greaves

Jimmy Greaves: I've cheated a little by selecting Billy Wright, who was involved on the production side. The Editor insisted on me taking the No.12 shirt, although my two stand-by selections were David Icke and Frank Bough. David was a goalkeeper with Coventry and Hereford until arthritis forced his premature retirement. Frank played at centre-half for Oxford University against Cambridge at Wembley. Granada commentator Martin Tyler was another on my short-list. He was a good-class centre-forward with Corinthian Casuals but I think he would bow the knee to the forwards in this team!

MANAGERS UNITED

A team of internationals who have played for and managed First Division clubs since 1946

1 Gil Merrick (E)
2 Alf Ramsey (E) (capt)
3 Tommy Docherty (S)
4 Bobby Robson (E)
5 Jackie Charlton (E)
6 Terry Neill (NI)
7 Alan Mullery (E)
8 Don Revie (E)
9 Brian Clough (E)
10 Dave Mackay (S)
11 Billy Bingham (NI)
Sub: Bill Nicholson (E)

WEST HAM UNITED UNITED

A team of West Ham players who became League managers

1 Martin Peters**
2 John Bond
3 John Lyall
4 Frank O'Farrell
5 Ken Brown
6 Malcolm Allison
7 Dave Sexton
8 Jimmy Bloomfield
9 Ron Tindall
10 Geoff Hurst
11 Noel Cantwell (capt)
Sub: Andy Nelson

**Martin Peters played in ten different numbered shirts for West Ham, including once as emergency goalkeeper

PAUL DANIELS'S DREAM TEAM

1 Gordon Banks
2 Terry Cooper
3 Ray Wilson
4 Danny Blanchflower (capt)
5 John Charles
6 Duncan Edwards
7 George Best
8 Peter Doherty
9 Bobby Charlton
10 Kenny Dalglish
11 Tom Finney
Sub: Paul Madeley

'You're going to like this team. Not a lot but you will like it! I know I'm playing Terry Cooper out of position at right-back but he had such skill that I'm sure he would be just as effective on the right side of the defence. In Paul Madeley I've got a substitute who can fill in at any position. In a word, this team is magic!'

Paul Daniels, Britain's No.1 man of magic, was born in Middlesbrough and, as any North-Easterner will tell you, there's no way you can grow up on Teesside without being a football fan.

MINERS WHO BECAME MAJOR STARS

Footballers who started out with colliery teams

1 **Ted Sagar** (Thorne Colliery)
2 **Tom Garrett** (Horden Colliery)
3 **Cyril Knowles** (Monckton Colliery)
4 **Stan Anderson** (Horden Colliery) (capt)
5 **Charlie Williams†** (Upton Colliery)
6 **Tommy Cummings†** (Hylton Colliery)
7 **Colin Bell** (Horden Colliery)
8 **Jimmy Hagan** (Usworth Colliery)
9 **Harold Hassall** (Astley Colliery)
10 **Ernie Taylor** (Hylton Colliery)
11 **Gordon Harris** (Firebeck Colliery)
Sub: Malcolm Musgrove† (Lynemouth Colliery)

A TEAM TO RUN THROUGH BRICK WALLS

Competitive players who had a win-at-all-costs attitude to go with their skill

1 Gary Sprake (W)
2 Peter Storey (E)
3 Cyril Knowles (E)
4 Billy Bremner (S)
5 Jimmy Scoular (S)
6 Norman Hunter (E)
7 Cliff Jones (W)
8 Tommy Smith (E)
9 Nat Lofthouse (E)
10 Dave Mackay (S) (capt)
11 Peter McParland (NI)
Sub: Nobby Stiles (E)

THE FIRST POST-WAR ENGLAND TEAM SELECTED BY WALTER WINTERBOTTOM (& selection committee)

1 Frank Swift
2 Laurie Scott
3 George Hardwick (capt)
4 Billy Wright
5 Neil Franklin
6 Henry Cockburn
7 Tom Finney
8 Raich Carter
9 Tommy Lawton
10 Wilf Mannion
11 Bobby Langton

Result: England 7, Northern Ireland 2. Venue: Belfast. 28 Sept 1946. Scorers: Carter, Mannion (3), Finney, Lawton, Langton

WALTER WINTERBOTTOM'S FINAL SELECTION

1 Ron Springett
2 Jimmy Armfield (capt)
3 Graham Shaw
4 Bobby Moore
5 Brian Labone
6 Ron Flowers
7 John Connelly
8 Freddie Hill
9 Alan Peacock
10 Jimmy Greaves
11 Bobby Tambling

Results: England 4, Wales 0. Venue: Wembley. 21 Nov 1962
Scorers: Connelly, Peacock (2), Greaves

RONNIE CORBETT'S DREAM TEAM

1 Gordon Banks
2 Johnny Carey
3 Arthur Albiston
4 Dave Mackay (capt)
5 Billy Wright
6 Duncan Edwards
7 Tom Finney
8 John White
9 Bobby Charlton
10 Jimmy Greaves
11 Billy Liddell
Sub: Willie Bauld

'I have indulged the Scotsman in me with the choice of Willie Bauld as substitute, even though he never played in English League football. He was a genius of a centre-forward with Hearts, who lit up my childhood, and he was a particular delight to my father who was a very good judge of football and had a *feel* for the really skilful, gentle Scottish players. I have insisted on including the one and only Jimmy Greaves even though he often caused torment to Scottish defenders. He and the late, great John White, along with Dave 'The Heart' Mackay, were marvellous to watch in that Super Spurs side of the 1960s.'

Ronnie Corbett used to train with Hearts as a schoolboy winger and dreamt of following a cousin of his into the Hearts first-team. But it was show business's gain and soccer's loss that he chose a career as an entertainer. He and Ronnie Barker go together as comfortably as Ramsey and Eckersley. . .Cohen and Wilson. . .Scott and Harwick. . . .

Sir Alf Ramsey, a great player and a great manager

ALF RAMSEY'S FIRST ENGLAND SELECTION

1 **Ron Springett**
2 **Jimmy Armfield (capt)**
3 **Ron Henry**
4 **Bobby Moore**
5 **Brian Labone**
6 **Ron Flowers**
7 **John Connelly**
8 **Bobby Tambling**
9 **Bobby Smith**
10 **Jimmy Greaves**
11 **Bobby Charlton**

Result: England 2, France 5. Venue: Paris. 27 Feb 1963
Scorers: Smith and Tambling

SIR ALF RAMSEY'S FINAL ENGLAND SELECTION

1 **Phil Parkes**
2 **David Nish**
3 **Mike Pejic**
4 **Martin Dobson**
5 **Dave Watson**
6 **Colin Todd**
7 **Stan Bowles**
8 **Mike Channon**
9 **Malcolm Macdonald**
10 **Trevor Brooking**
11 **Martin Peters (capt)**
Sub: Alan Ball

Result: England 0, Portugal 0. Venue: Lisbon. 3 April 1974

DON REVIE'S FIRST ENGLAND SELECTION

1 Ray Clemence
2 Paul Madeley
3 Emlyn Hughes (capt)
4 Martin Dobson
5 Dave Watson
6 Norman Hunter
7 Colin Bell
8 Gerry Francis
9 Frank Worthington
10 Mike Channon
11 Kevin Keegan
Sub: Trevor Brooking and Dave Thomas

Result: England 3, Czechoslovakia 0. Venue: Wembley. 30 Oct 1974. Scorers: Channon, Bell (2)

DON REVIE'S FINAL ENGLAND SELECTION

1 Ray Clemence
2 Phil Neal
3 Trevor Cherry
4 Brian Greenhoff
5 Dave Watson
6 Emlyn Hughes
7 Kevin Keegan (capt)
8 Mike Channon
9 Stuart Pearson
10 Ray Wilkins
11 Brian Talbot

Result: England 0, Uruguay 0. Venue: Montevideo. 15 June 1977

RON GREENWOOD'S FIRST ENGLAND SELECTION

1 **Ray Clemence**
2 **Phil Neal**
3 **Trevor Cherry**
4 **Terry McDermott**
5 **Dave Watson**
6 **Emlyn Hughes (capt)**
7 **Kevin Keegan**
8 **Mike Channon**
9 **Trevor Francis**
10 **Ray Kennedy**
11 **Ian Callaghan**
Subs: Gordon Hill and Ray Wilkins

Result: England 0, Switzerland 0. Venue: Wembley. 7 Sept 1977

RON GREENWOOD'S FINAL ENGLAND SELECTION

1 **Peter Shilton**
2 **Mick Mills (capt)**
3 **Kenny Sansom**
4 **Phil Thompson**
5 **Terry Butcher**
6 **Bryan Robson**
7 **Graham Rix**
8 **Trevor Francis**
9 **Paul Mariner**
10 **Tony Woodcock**
11 **Ray Wilkins**
Subs: Trevor Brooking and Kevin Keegan

Result: England 0, Spain 0. Venue: Madrid. 5 July 1982

SECTION FOUR

NAME GAMES

THE ELEVEN RONNIES

1 **Ron Springett**
2 **Ron Staniforth**
3 **Ron Henry**
4 **Ron Clayton**
5 **Ron Yeats**
6 **Ron Burgess (capt)**
7 **Ron Whelan**
8 **Ronnie Allen**
9 **Ron Davies**
10 **Ron Saunders†**
11 **Ronnie Rees**
Sub: Ron Flowers

THE TOP JOHNNYS

1 **John Phillips**
2 **John Gidman**
3 **Johnny Carey**
4 **John Hollins**
5 **John Charles**
6 **John White**
7 **Johnny Hancocks**
8 **Johnny Giles**
9 **Johnny Byrne**
10 **Johnny Haynes (capt)**
11 **John Robertson**
Sub: John Wark

THE BOBBY DAZZLERS

1 **Bob Wilson**
2 **Bobby Thomson**
3 **Bob McNab**
4 **Bobby Robson**
5 **Bobby Evans**
6 **Bobby Moore (capt)**
7 **Bobby Murdoch**
8 **Bobby Tambling**
9 **Bobby Smith**
10 **Bobby Collins**
11 **Bobby Charlton**
Sub: Bobby Moncur

A JAMBOREE OF JIMMYS

1 **Jimmy Rimmer**
2 **Jimmy Armfield (capt)**
3 **Jim Langley**
4 **Jimmy Scoular**
5 **Jimmy Dickinson**
6 **Jim Baxter**
7 **Jimmy Johnstone**
8 **Jimmy Greaves****
9 **Jimmy Melia**
10 **Jimmy McIlroy**
11 **Jimmy Mullen**
Sub: Jimmy Adamson†

**Editor's selection

AN ALLIANCE OF ALANS

1 **Alan Hodgkinson**
2 **Alan Hansen**
3 **Alan Kennedy†**
4 **Alan Mullery (capt)**
5 **Allan Hunter**
6 **Alan Devonshire**
7 **Alan Ball**
8 **Allan Clarke**
9 **Alan Peacock**
10 **Alan Gilzean**
11 **Alan Hinton**
Sub: Alan Sunderland

Alan Ball, a skilled and totally committed player

A DIVISION OF DAVIDS

1 David Harvey
2 David Hay
3 David Webb†
4 David O'Leary
5 Dave Watson
6 Dave Mackay (capt)
7 David McCreery
8 David Johnson
9 David Herd
10 Davie Gibson
11 David Armstrong
Sub: David Fairclough†

THE TOMMY GUNNERS

1 Tommy Lawrence
2 Tommy Wright
3 Tommy Gemmell
4 Tommy Docherty (capt)
5 Tommy Cummings†
6 Tommy Smith
7 Tommy Hutchison
8 Tommy Taylor
9 Tommy Lawton
10 Tommy Thompson
11 Tom Finney
Sub: Tom Garrett

THE FRANK BRIGADE

1 **Frank Swift**
2 **Frank Lampard**
3 **Frank Gray**
4 **Frank McLintock (capt)**
5 **Frank Brennan**
6 **Frank Munro**
7 **Frank Broome**
8 **Frank Stapleton**
9 **Frank Wignall**
10 **Frank Worthington**
11 **Frank Blunstone**
Sub: Frank Carrodus†

THE KING BILLYS

1 **Bill Brown**
2 **Bill Foulkes**
3 **Bill Eckersley**
4 **Bill McGarry**
5 **Billy Wright (capt)**
6 **Bill Slater**
7 **Billy Bingham**
8 **Billy Bremner**
9 **Billy Hamilton**
10 **Billy Steel**
11 **Billy Liddell**
Sub: Bill Perry

A GORGE OF GEORGES

1 George Farm
2 George Cohen
3 George Hardwick (capt)
4 George Burley
5 George Curtis†
6 George Mulhall
7 George Armstrong
8 George Best
9 George Graham
10 George Eastham
11 George Robb
Sub: George Hannah†

TERRY'S ALL GOLD

1 Terry Webster†
2 Terry Butcher
3 Terry Cooper
4 Terry Hennessey
5 Terry Neill (capt)
6 Terry Yorath
7 Terry Paine
8 Terry McDermott
9 Terry Bly†
10 Terry Venables
11 Terry Medwin
Sub: Terry Mancini

TWENTY TEAMS TO MAKE AN INITIAL IMPACT

A

1 John Anderson (S)
2 Viv Anderson (E)
3 Jimmy Armfield (E) (capt)
4 Stan Anderson (E)
5 Jimmy Adamson (E)†
6 Ivor Allchurch (W)
7 Osvaldo Ardiles (Arg)
8 Ronnie Allen (E)
9 Jeff Astle (E)
10 John Atyeo (E)
11 Bertie Auld (S)
Sub: David Armstrong (E)

B

1 Gordon Banks (E)
2 Walley Barnes (W)
3 Roger Byrne (E)
4 Danny Blanchflower (NI) (capt)
5 Ron Burgess
6 Martin Buchan (S)
7 Alan Ball (E)
8 Colin Bell (E)
9 Johnny Byrne (E)
10 Peter Broadbent (E)
11 George Best (NI)
Sub: Billy Bremner (S)

C

1 Ray Clemence (E)
2 George Cohen (E)
3 Terry Cooper (E)
4 Pat Crerand (S)
5 Jackie Charlton (E)
6 John Carey (Ei) (capt)
7 Steve Coppell (E)
8 Raich Carter (E)
9 John Charles (W)
10 Brian Clough (E)
11 Bobby Charlton (E)
Sub: Bobby Collins (S)

D

1 Ted Ditchburn (E)
2 Tony Dunne (Ei)
3 Willie Donachie (S)
4 Tommy Docherty (S) (capt)
5 Ray Daniel (W)
6 Jimmy Dickinson (E)
7 Bryan Douglas (E)
8 Kenny Dalglish (S)
9 Ron Davies (W)
10 Derek Dougan (NI)
11 Peter Doherty (NI)
Sub: Alan Durban (W)

E

1 Fred Else (E)†
2 Alex Elder (NI)
3 Bill Eckersley (E)
4 Bobby Evans (S) (capt)
5 Mike England (W)
6 Duncan Edwards (E)
7 Billy Elliott (E)
8 George Edwards (W)
9 Alun Evans (E)†
10 George Eastham (E)
11 Tom Eglington (NI)
Sub: Brian Evans (W)

F

1 George Farm (S)
2 Bill Foulkes (E) (capt)
3 Alex Forsyth (S)
4 Alex Forbes (S)
5 Neil Franklin (E)
6 Ron Flowers (E)
7 Charlie Fleming (S)
8 Trevor Francis (E)
9 Trevor Ford (W)
10 Jack Froggatt (E)
11 Tom Finney (E)
Sub: Redfern Froggatt

G

1 Harry Gregg (NI)
2 Tommy Gemmell (S)
3 Frank Gray (S)
4 George Graham (S)
5 Brian Greenhoff (E)
6 Jimmy Gabriel (S) (capt)
7 Archie Gemmill (S)
8 Jimmy Greaves (E)**
9 Alan Gilzean (S)
10 Johnny Giles (Ei)
11 Eddie Gray (S)
Sub: Andy Gray (S)

**Editor's selection

H

1 Eddie Hopkinson (E)
2 Don Howe (E)
3 Emlyn Hughes (E)
4 Glen Hoddle (E)
5 Allan Hunter (Ei)
6 Norman Hunter (E)
7 Johnny Hancocks (E)
8 Roger Hunt (E)
9 Geoff Hurst (E)
10 Johnny Haynes (E) (capt)
11 Steve Heighway (Ei)
Sub: Mel Hopkins (W)

J

1 Pat Jennings (NI)
2 Bill Jones (E)
3 Joey Jones (W)
4 Craig Johnston (SA)†
5 Harry Johnston (E) (capt)
6 Tommy Jackson (NI)
7 Jimmy Johnstone (S)
8 David Johnson (E)
9 Joe Jordan (S)
10 Bobby Johnstone (S)
11 Cliff Jones (W)
Sub: Leighton James (W)

K

1 Jack Kelsey (W)
2 Joe Kinnear (Ei)
3 Cyril Knowles (E)
4 Tony Kay (E)
5 Tony Knapp (E)†
6 Howard Kendall (E)
7 Kevin Keegan (E) (capt)
8 Brian Kidd (E)
9 Derek Kevan (E)
10 Ray Kennedy (E)
11 Steve Kindon (E)†
Sub: Hugh Kelly (S)

L

1 Tommy Lawrence (S)
2 Chris Lawler (E)
3 Jim Langley (E)
4 Peter Lorimer (S)
5 Brian Labone (E) (capt)
6 Mark Lawrenson (Ei)
7 Francis Lee (E)
8 Denis Law (S)
9 Tommy Lawton (E)
10 Nat Lofthouse (E)
11 Billy Liddell (S)
Sub: Bob Latchford (E)

M

1 Gil Merrick (E)
2 Mick Mills (E)
3 Joe Mercer (E)
4 Alan Mullery (E)
5 Bobby Moncur (S)
6 Bobby Moore (E) (capt)
7 Stanley Matthews (E)
8 Stan Mortensen (E)
9 Paul Mariner (E)
10 Wilf Mannion (E)
11 Jackie Milburn (E)
Sub: Paul Madeley (E)

Mc

1 Colin McDonald (E)
2 Bob McNab (E)
3 Eddie McCreadie (S)
4 Frank McLintock (S)
5 Roy McFarland (E)
6 Dave Mackay (S) (capt)
7 Lou Macari (S)
8 Terry McDermott (E)
9 Malcolm Macdonald (E)
10 Jimmy McIlroy (NI)
11 Peter McParland (NI)
Sub: Sammy McIlroy (NI)

N

1 Ken Nethercott (E)†
2 Phil Neal (E)
3 Keith Newton (E)
4 Bill Nicholson (E)
5 Maurice Norman (E)
6 Mel Nurse (W)
7 Terry Neill (NI) (capt)
8 Jimmy Nicholson (NI)
9 Peter Nicholas (W)
10 Johnny Nicholls (E)†
11 Sammy Nelson (NI)
Sub: David Nish (E)

O

1 John Osborne (E)†
2 Russell Osman (E)
3 David O'Leary (Ei)
4 Frank O'Farrell (Ei)
5 Syd Owen (E) (capt)
6 Alan Oakes (E)†
7 Gary Owen (E)†
8 John O'Hara (S)
9 Peter Osgood (E)
10 Martin O'Neill (NI)
11 Mike O'Grady (E)
Sub: Liam O'Kane (NI)

P

1 Phil Parkes (E)
2 Alex Parker (S)
3 Mike Pejic (E)
4 Martin Peters (E)
5 Steve Perryman (E)
6 Roy Paul (W) (capt)
7 Terry Paine (E)
8 Stuart Pearson (E)
9 Fred Pickering (E)
10 Stan Pearson (E)
11 Bill Perry (E)
Sub: Leighton Phillips (W)

R

1 Jimmy Rimmer (E)
2 Alf Ramsey (E) (capt)
3 Peter Rodrigues (W)
4 Bobby Robson (E)
5 John Roberts (W)
6 Bryan Robson (E)
7 Don Revie (E)
8 Cyrille Regis (E)
9 Joe Royle (E)
10 Jack Rowley (E)
11 John Robertson (S)
Sub: Ian Rush (W)

S

1 Frank Swift (E)
2 Tommy Smith (E)
3 Kenny Sansom (E)
4 Nobby Stiles (E)
5 Peter Swan (E)
6 Jimmy Scoular (S) (capt)
7 Graeme Souness (S)
8 Ian St John (S)
9 Bobby Smith (E)
10 Len Shackleton (E)
11 Billy Steel (S)
Sub: Bill Slater (E)

T

1 Bert Trautmann (WG)†
2 Bobby Thomson (E)
3 Rod Thomas (W)
4 Brian Talbot (E)
5 Phil Thompson (E) (capt)
6 Mickey Thomas (W)
7 Peter Thompson (E)
8 John Toshack (W)
9 Tommy Taylor (E)
10 Ernie Taylor (E)
11 Bobby Tambling (E)
Sub: Derek Tapscott (W)

W

1 Bert Williams (E)
2 Stuart Williams (W)
3 Ray Wilson (E)
4 Billy Wright (E) (capt)
5 Dave Watson (E)
6 John Wark (E)
7 Frank Worthington (E)
8 John White (S)
9 Peter Withe (E)
10 Ray Wilkins (E)
11 Tony Woodcock (E)
Sub: Dennis Wilshaw (E)

Tony Woodcock (left), in action for England

MALCOLM ALLISON'S DREAM TEAM

1 Peter Shilton
2 Mike Summerbee
3 Ken Sansom
4 Duncan Edwards
5 John Charles
6 Bobby Moore (capt)
7 Stanley Matthews
8 George Best
9 Tommy Lawton
10 Peter Doherty
11 Tom Finney
Sub: Kevin Keegan

> 'I wouldn't have liked to play against a team of such all-round quality, power and class – but I would love to have managed them! Mike Summerbee would wear the No.2 shirt but have a 'free' role to go wherever he could best assist the team.'

Malcolm Allison is recognized by many people in football as one of the greatest coaches in the game. His flair and invention have been on show with Plymouth, Manchester City, Crystal Palace, Sporting Lisbon and Middlesborough. He was an outstanding centre-half with West Ham until illness forced his premature retirement.

THE MIGHTY SMITHS

1 **George Smith** (Notts County)
2 **Wilf Smith** (Sheffield Wednesday)
3 **Lionel Smith (E)** (Arsenal)
4 **Tommy Smith (E)** (Liverpool) (capt)
5 **Trevor Smith (E)** (Birmingham City)
6 **Seph Smith (E)** (Leicester City)
7 **Gordon Smith (S)** (Brighton)
8 **Jim Smith (S)** (Newcastle United)
9 **Bobby Smith (E)** (Spurs)
10 **John Smith** (West Ham, Spurs, etc)
11 **Leslie Smith (E)** (Aston Villa)
Sub: Jim Smith (Preston)

KEEPING UP WITH THE JONESES

1 **Keith Jones (W)** (Aston Villa)
2 **Gordon Jones** (Middlesbrough)
3 **Joey Jones (W)** (Liverpool)
4 **Sam Jones (NI)** (Blackpool)
5 **Tom Jones (W)** (Everton)
6 **Bill Jones (E)** (Liverpool)
7 **Barrie Jones (W)** (Swansea) (capt)
8 **Ernie Jones (W)** (Spurs)
9 **Mick Jones (E)** (Leeds United)
10 **Bryn Jones (W)** (Arsenal)
11 **Cliff Jones (W)** (Spurs)
Sub: Dave Jones (W) (Norwich)

BROWNS OF RENOWN

1 **Bill Brown (S)** (Spurs)
2 **Bobby Brown** (Workington)
3 **Alex (Sandy) Brown** (Everton)
4 **Hugh Brown (S)** (Torquay)
5 **Ken Brown (E)** (West Ham) (capt)
6 **Stan Brown** (Fulham)
7 **John Brown (NI)** (Ipswich Town)
8 **Tony Brown (E)** (West Brom)
9 **Eddy Brown** (Birmingham City)
10 **Allan Brown (S)** (Blackpool)
11 **Alistair Brown** (West Brom)
Sub: **Laurie Brown** (Arsenal)

A TEAM OF WINNING WILSONS

1 **Bob Wilson (S)** (Arsenal)
2 **Joe Wilson** (Nottingham Forest)
3 **Ray Wilson (E)** (Everton) (capt)
4 **Billy Wilson** (Burnley)
5 **Bev Wilson** (Barrow)
6 **Les Wilson** (Wolves)
7 **Davie Wilson** (Preston)
8 **Alex Wilson** (Portsmouth)
9 **Tom Wilson** (Nottingham Forest)
10 **Eugene Wilson** (Stockport County)
11 **Ian Wilson** (Rotherham)
Sub: **Andy Wilson** (Scunthorpe)

Ray Wilson, an elegant left-back for Huddersfield, Everton and England

A TEAM OF THOMMOS

1 **George Thompson** (Preston)
2 **Rod Thomas (W)** (Derby)
3 **Bobby Thomson (E)** (Wolves)
4 **Phil Thompson (E)** (Liverpool) (capt)
5 **Ken Thomson** (Stoke)
6 **Mike Thomas (W)** (Stoke)
7 **Dave Thomas (E)** (Burnley)
8 **Danny Thomas** (Coventry)
9 **Tommy Thompson (E)** (Aston Villa/Preston)
10 **David Thomas (W)** (Swansea)
11 **Peter Thompson (E)** (Liverpool)
Sub: Gary Thompson (Coventry WBA)

A TAYLOR-MADE TEAM

1 **Peter Taylor** (Middlesbrough)
2 **Gerry Taylor** (Wolves)
3 **Tony Taylor** (Crystal Palace)
4 **Tommy Taylor** (West Ham)
5 **Jim Taylor (E)** (Fulham)
6 **Phil Taylor (E)** (Liverpool) (capt)
7 **Alan Taylor** (West Ham)
8 **Gordon Taylor** (Bolton)
9 **Tommy Taylor (E)** (Manchester United)
10 **Ernie Taylor (E)** (Blackpool)
11 **Peter Taylor (E)** (Crystal Palace/Spurs)
Sub: Ken Taylor (Blackburn)

DAVID ESSEX'S DREAM TEAM

1 Willie Whitelaw
2 Danny La Rue
3 Michael Foot
4 Sir John Gielgud
5 Charlie Drake (capt)
6 Princess Margaret
7 Spike Milligan
8 Brian Clough
9 Tommy Cooper
10 Ronnie Biggs
11 Cyril Smith
Sub: Elton John

‘They may not win many matches, but it would be interesting to see them in action! To be serious for a moment, how about the West Ham team that won the 1964 FA Cup as a dream combination – Standen, Bond, Burkett, Bovington, Brown, Moore, Brabrook, Boyce, Byrne, Hurst, Sissons. I think it was the only time an all-English team of players had won the Cup.’

David Essex was a schoolboy player with West Ham United when he was known as David Cook. He was good enough to make the grade as a professional, but from the moment he was spotted playing drums by his manager, Derek Bowman, he accepted that football had to take a back seat to his show business career.

COMMENTATOR'S NIGHTMARE

A tongue-twisting team of players who have all appeared in Football League matches

1 **Radojko Avramovic** (Yugoslavia)
2 **Dzemal Hadziabdic** (Yugoslavia)
3 **Rickie Kwiatskowski** (England)
4 **Ryszard Kowenicki** (Poland)
5 **Ray Mielczarek** (Wales) (capt)
6 **Mickey Czuczman** (England)
7 **Edouard Wojtczak** (Poland)
8 **Anton Otulakowski** (England)
9 **Steve Wojciechowicz** (England)
10 **Dick Kryzwickie** (Wales)
11 **Mark Dziadulewicz** (England)
Sub: Albert Uytenbogaardt (South Africa)

TERRY LAWLESS'S DREAM TEAM

1 Ted Ditchburn
2 Alf Ramsey
3 Roger Byrne
4 Bobby Moore (capt)
5 John Charles
6 Duncan Edwards
7 Stanley Matthews
8 George Best
9 Tommy Lawton
10 Jimmy Greaves
11 Tom Finney
Sub: Martin Peters

'I was tempted to pick the West Ham team that won promotion to the First Division back in 1958, and I'd at least like you to give them a mention – Gregory, Bond, Cantwell, Malcolm, Brown, Allison or Moore, Grice, John Smith, Keeble, Dick and Musgrove. I've selected Martin Peters as substitute because he could slot into virtually any position. I remember him even playing in goal at West Ham. You'll struggle to find a better forward line. Football fans would walk a million miles to see this lot in action, particularly Best and Greaves. What a combination!'

Terry Lawless is Britain's greatest ever boxing manager who has steered four fighters – John Stracey, Maurice Hope, Jim Watt and Charlie Magri – to world titles. He takes a keen interest in the fortunes of West Ham and numbers John Lyall, Dave Sexton and Bryan 'Pop' Robson among his circle of friends.

SECTION FIVE

THE POLL TOPPERS

HEROES OF THE HEROES

One hundred current professionals were asked to name their boyhood heroes. This was the 'Top Ten' list:

1. **George Best**
2. **Bobby Charlton**
3. **Denis Law**
4. **Jimmy Greaves**
5. **Bobby Moore**
6. **Geoff Hurst**
7. **Roger Hunt**
8. **Gordon Banks**
9. **Francis Lee**
10. **Alan Ball**

Jimmy Greaves: It's fascinating to notice that all of them bar Bobby Moore were forwards and also that they were at their peak in the 1960s. My boyhood heroes were also forwards – Len Shackleton, Stanley Matthews, Tom Finney, Raich Carter and Tommy Lawton.

Kenny Dalglish, one of the modern masters

THE PLAYERS' PLAYERS

One hundred current professionals were asked to name the current League players they most admire. This was the 'Top Ten' list:

1 Kenny Dalglish
2 Bryan Robson
3 Kevin Keegan
4 Glenn Hoddle
5 Trevor Brooking
6 Peter Shilton
7 Graeme Souness
8 Trevor Francis
9 Mark Lawrenson
10 Ray Clemence

Jimmy Greaves: My list would be very similar. The one addition I would make is goalkeeper Pat Jennings, football's man for all seasons.

KING OF CLUBS

One hundred current professionals were asked (in confidence) which club they would most like to play for if they had a free choice. This was the 'Top Ten' list:

1 Manchester United
2 Liverpool
3 Spurs
4 Arsenal
5 Manchester City
6 Aston Villa
7 Everton
8 Nottingham Forest
9 Ipswich Town
10 West Ham United

Jimmy Greaves: We had to give the players a second choice to help us get a 'Top Ten' list. There were only six clubs after the first count! If I could play it again, Sam, I'd plump for a full career with Spurs.

THE TEN HAPPIEST HUNTING GROUNDS

One hundred current professionals were asked to name their favourite League grounds. This was the 'Top Ten' list:

1 Old Trafford
2 Anfield
3 Villa Park
4 Highbury
5 Maine Road
6 White Hart Lane
7 Goodison
8 Portman Road
9 Upton Park
10 St Andrews

Jimmy Greaves: I would always have to claim White Hart Lane as my favourite hunting ground. The Ipswich ground at

Portman Road was another that I always enjoyed playing at because the pitch was so beautifully kept. It was like playing on a bowling green. Anfield had a marvellous atmosphere thanks to the Kop fans, but I can't pretend to have enjoyed my visits there. I was never once on the winning side.

The ground I rate above all others for having a special magic 'feel' is Villa Park where you get a great sense of history the moment you step through the impressive entrance. Sheffield Wednesday's ground at Hillsborough is another that I would put in my personal Top Ten.

DENNIS WATERMAN'S DREAM TEAM

1 Gordon Banks
2 Terry Cooper
3 Roger Byrne
4 Billy Bremner
5 Billy Wright (capt)
6 Duncan Edwards
7 Tom Finney
8 Martin Peters
9 Bobby Charlton
10 Denis Law
11 George Best
Sub: Kenny Dalglish

'I will never be rude about a manager's selection again. I found this an almost impossible task. I have selected Byrne and Edwards simply because of the dreamy look that comes into the eyes of experts when their names are mentioned. I'm just a bit too young to have seen them play. I can hear the reader asking. . ."Where's Moore. . . John Charles. . .Keegan. . .Blanchflower. . .Stiles. . .Allchurch. . .Macdonald. . .Ball. . .Osgood. . .Marsh. . .et al. . .?" I think I'll stick to acting.'

Minder star Dennis Waterman comes from a sporting family. His brother, Peter, is a former European and British welterweight boxing champion. He is a good-quality footballer, as he proved when making the acclaimed television play 'The World Cup – A Captain's Tale'.

THE PERSON THEY'D MOST LIKE TO MEET

One hundred current footballers were asked to name the person they would most like to meet. This was the 'Top Ten' list:

1 **The Princess of Wales**
2 **The Queen**
3 **Paul McCartney**
4 **David Bowie**
5 **Prince Andrew**
6 **John McEnroe**
7 **The Pope**
8 **Pele**
9 **Jack Nicklaus**
10 **Muhammad Ali**

THE SPORTSMAN THEY'D MOST LIKE TO BE

One hundred current footballers were asked to name the sportsman (not footballers) they would most like to be if they were not themselves. This was the 'Top Ten' list:

1 **John McEnroe**
2 **Jack Nicklaus**
3 **Lester Piggott**
4 **Ian Botham**
5 **Sevvy Ballesteros**
6 **Sebastian Coe**
7 **Steve Davis**
8 **Daley Thompson**
9 **Jimmy Connors**
10 **Larry Holmes**

Jimmy Greaves: It's interesting to see how lawn tennis has taken over as the No.1 international sport. I'm not surprised when you consider how much money these men with the golden arm pick up. In my young playing days I would have elected to have been Lester Piggott, Rod Laver or Arnold Palmer, my three all-time favourite sports stars.

John McEnroe, a keen soccer player before becoming the man with the golden arm

TEN NON-FOOTBALLING DISLIKES OF FOOTBALLERS

One hundred current professionals were asked to name their chief dislikes. This was the 'Top Ten' list:

1 **Flying**
2 **Hanging about airport lounges**
3 **Bumptious, boring officials**
4 **Foreign food**
5 **Bad write-ups**
6 **Official banquets**
7 **Isolated hotels**
8 **Formal dress**
9 **Long coach rides**
10 **Hangers-on**

TEN NON-FOOTBALLING LIKES OF FOOTBALLERS

Ten current professional footballers were asked to name their chief non-sporting likes. This was the 'Top Ten' list:

1 **Win bonuses**
2 **Fast cars**
3 **Bird watching**
4 **Parties**
5 **A good drink**
6 **Card schools**
7 **Watching TV**
8 **Casual clothes**
9 **Travel**
10 **VIP fans**

PETE MURRAY'S DREAM TEAM

1 Gordon Banks
2 Alf Ramsey
3 Eddie Hapgood
4 Bryan Robson
5 Jackie Charlton
6 Dave Mackay
7 Stanley Matthews
8 Denis Law
9 John Charles
10 Liam Brady
11 Tom Finney
Sub: Trevor Francis

'I resisted the temptation to select my eleven favourite Arsenal players because it would have cost me sleep trying to decide which ones to leave out. I settled for this balanced team, with just Eddie Hapgood and Liam Brady included from my army of Highbury heroes.'

Pete Murray, radio show host, TV compere and actor, has two major hobbies – watching Arsenal in the winter and lawn tennis in the summer. He shares with Jimmy Young a life-long attachment to Arsenal and both are walking record books on the history of the Highbury club.

HOBBIES OF THE HEROES

One hundred current professionals were asked their hobbies away from football. This was the 'Top Ten' list:

1 Golf
2 Lawn tennis
3 Driving
4 Listening to records
5 Snooker
6 Watching TV
7 Horse racing
8 The cinema
9 Disco dancing
10 Fishing

A TEAM FOR ALL SEASONS

One hundred current professionals were asked to name their all-time all-star British football team. To avoid embarrassment (particularly my own), I asked not to be considered. This was the poll-topping team (4–2–4):

Gordon Banks
Danny McGrain
Jackie Charlton
Bobby Moore
Terry Cooper
Bryan Robson
Bobby Charlton
Kevin Keegan
Denis Law
Kenny Dalglish
George Best
Sub: Dave Mackay

Jackie Charlton (right) got into the Team for All Seasons by a neck

SECTION SIX

TOP TEN STATISTICS**
compiled by Malcolm Rowley

INTERNATIONAL CAPS

'Top Ten' list plus tables for England, Northern Ireland, Scotland and Wales. International career span in brackets.

1	**Bobby Moore** (England, 1962–73)	108
2	**Bobby Charlton** (England, 1958–70)	106
3	**Billy Wright** (England, 1946–59)	105
4	**Pat Jennings** (Northern Ireland, 1964–)	95
5	**Kenny Dalglish** (Scotland, 1971–)	90
6	**Tom Finney** (England, 1946–58)	76
7	**Gordon Banks** (England, 1963–72)	73
8	**Alan Ball** (England, 1965–75)	72
9	**Sammy McIlroy** (Northern Ireland, 1972)	69
10	**Ivor Allchurch** (Wales, 1950–66)	68

**All facts and Internationals up to 1 August 1983, unless otherwise stated

TOMMY CANNON'S DREAM TEAM

1 Gordon Banks
2 Terry Cooper
3 Ray Wilson
4 Nobby Stiles
5 Billy Wright (capt)
6 Bobby Moore
7 Alan Ball
8 Kevin Keegan
9 Bobby Charlton
10 Denis Law
11 George Best
Sub: Dave Mackay

'If you could have got this combination together it would have been a world-beating team. It would frighten the life out of the opposition to see a player of Dave Mackay's calibre sitting on the substitute's bench waiting to join the action!'

Tommy Cannon and his partner Bobby Ball are now firmly established as kings of comedy. Oldham-born Tommy is a keen football follower with a leaning towards Manchester United, as his choice of four old Trafford idols will indicate.

INTERNATIONAL CAPS – ENGLAND

1	**Bobby Moore** (1962–73)	108
2	**Bobby Charlton** (1958–70)	106
3	**Billy Wright** (1946–59)	105
4	**Tom Finney** (1946–58)	76
5	**Gordon Banks** (1963–72)	73
6	**Alan Ball** (1965–75)	72
7	**Martin Peters** (1966–74)	67
8	**Dave Watson** (1974–82)	65
=9	**Ray Wilson** (1960–68)	63
	Kevin Keegan (1973–82)	63

INTERNATIONAL CAPS – NORTHERN IRELAND

1	**Pat Jennings** (1964–)	99
2	**Sammy McIlroy** (1972–)	69
3	**Terry Neill** (1961–73)	59
4	**Martin O'Neill** (1972–)	57
=5	**Billy Bingham** (1951–64)	56
	Danny Blanchflower (1950–63)	56
	Jimmy Nicholl (1976)	56
8	**Jimmy McIlroy** (1952–66)	55
9	**Sammy Nelson** (1970–)	51
10	**Bryan Hamilton** (1969–80)	50

Pat Jennings, a magnificent last line of defence

INTERNATIONAL CAPS – SCOTLAND

1	**Kenny Dalglish** (1971–)	90
2	**Danny McGrain** (1973–)	62
3	**Denis Law** (1958–74)	55
4	**Billy Bremner** (1965–75)	54
5	**George Young** (1948–57)	53
6	**Joe Jordan** (1973–)	52
7	**Alan Rough** (1976–)	51
8	**Asa Hartford** (1972–)	50
9	**Bobby Evans** (1948–60)	48
10	**John Greig** (1964–75)	44

INTERNATIONAL CAPS – WALES

1	**Ivor Allchurch** (1950–66)	68
=2	**Brian Flynn** (1974–)	59
	Cliff Jones (1954–69)	59
	Terry Yorath (1969–81)	59
5	**Leighton Phillips** (1971–)	58
6	**Leighton James** (1971–)	54
=7	**Dai Davies** (1975–)	52
	Joey Jones (1975–)	52
9	**John Mahoney** (1967–)	51
10	**Rod Thomas** (1967–78)	50

INTERNATIONAL GOALSCORERS

'Top Ten' list of British International goalscorers since 1946, plus tables for England, Northern Ireland, Scotland, and Wales. International career span in brackets.

		Goals	*Caps*
1	**Bobby Charlton** (England, 1958–70)	49	106
2	**Jimmy Greaves** (England, 1959–67)	44	57
=3	**Tom Finney** (England, 1946–58)	30	76
	Denis Law (Scotland, 1958–74)	30	55
	Nat Lofthouse (England, 1950–58)	30	33
6	**Kenny Dalglish** (Scotland, 1971–)	28	90
7	**Geoff Hurst** (England, 1966–72)	24	49
=8	**Trevor Ford** (Wales, 1947–56)	23	38
	Stan Mortensen (England, 1947–53)	23	25
=10	**Ivor Allchurch** (Wales, 1950–66)	22	68
	Lawrie Reilly (Scotland, 1948–57)	22	38

INTERNATIONAL GOAL-SCORERS – ENGLAND

		Goals	Caps
1	**Bobby Charlton** (1958–70)	49	106
2	**Jimmy Greaves** (1959–67)	44	57
=3	**Tom Finney** (1946–58)	30	76
	Nat Lofthouse (1950–58)	30	33
5	**Geoff Hurst** (1966–72)	24	49
6	**Stan Mortensen** (1947–53)	23	25
=7	**Mike Channon** (1972–77)	21	46
	Kevin Keegan (1973–82)	21	63
	Martin Peters (1966–74)	21	67
=10	**Johnny Haynes** (1955–62)	18	56
	Roger Hunt (1962–69)	18	34

INTERNATIONAL GOAL-SCORERS – NORTHERN IRELAND

		Goals	Caps
=1	**Gerry Armstrong** (1977–)	10	47
	Johnny Crossan (1959–67)	10	24
	Jimmy McIlroy (1952–66)	10	55
=4	**George Best** (1964–77)	9	37
	Billy Bingham (1951–64)	9	56
	Willie Irvine (1963–72)	9	23
	Peter McParland (1954–62)	9	34
8	**Derek Dougan** (1958–73)	8	43
=9	**Wilbur Cush** (1951–62)	7	26
	Billy McAdams (1954–1962)	7	15
	Sammy Wilson (1963–67)	7	12
	Martin O'Neill (1972–)	7	57

INTERNATIONAL GOAL-SCORERS – SCOTLAND

		Goals	*Caps*
1	**Denis Law** (1958–74)	30	55
2	**Kenny Dalglish** (1971–)	28	90
3	**Lawrie Reilly** (1948–57)	22	38
4	**Billy Steel** (1947–53)	13	30
5	**Alan Gilzean** (1963–71)	12	22
=6	**Joe Jordan** (1973–)	11	52
	Colin Stein (1968–73)	11	21
=8	**Bobby Collins** (1951–65)	10	31
	Bobby Johnstone (1951–56)	10	17
=10	**Jackie Mudie** (1956–58)	9	17
	Ian St John (1959–65)	9	21
	Davie Wilson (1960–65)	9	22

Denis Law, the 'Electric Heel' who brought showmanship as well as skill to the football pitch

INTERNATIONAL GOAL-SCORERS – WALES

		Goals	Caps
1	**Trevor Ford** (1947–56)	23	38
2	**Ivor Allchurch** (1950–66)	22	68
3	**Cliff Jones** (1954–69)	16	59
4	**John Charles** (1950–65)	15	38
5	**John Toshack** (1969–79)	12	40
6	**Leighton James** (1971–)	10	54
=7	**Ron Davies** (1964–74)	8	29
	Roy Vernon (1957–67)	8	32
=9	**Ian Walsh** (1979–)	7	18
	Brian Flynn (1974–)	7	59

LEAGUE APPEARANCES

'Top Ten' list of players who have made a record number of Football League appearances for one club:

		Total League Appearances
1	**John Trollope** (Swindon Town, 1960–80)	770
2	**Jimmy Dickinson** (Portsmouth, 1946–65)	764
3	**Roy Sproson** (Port Vale, 1950–72)	761
4	**Terry Paine** (Southampton, 1956–74)	713
5	**Ron Harris** (Chelsea, 1962–80)	655
6	**Ian Callaghan** (Liverpool, 1960–78)	640
=7	**Jackie Charlton** (Leeds United, 1953–73)	629
	Joe Shaw (Sheffield United, 1948–66)	629
9	**Bob McKinlay** (Nottingham Forest, 1951–70)	614
10	**Dave Blakey** (Chesterfield, 1948–67)	613

GOALSCORERS

'Top Ten' list of League goalscorers since 1940, plus tables of First, Second, Third and Fourth Division top scorers in a season:

		Clubs	Football League Goals
1	**Arthur Rowley** (1946–64)	West Brom, Fulham, Leicester City and Shrewsbury	434
2	**Jimmy Greaves** (1957–71)	Chelsea, Spurs and West Ham	357
3	**John Ayteo** (1951–65)	Bristol City	315
4	**Cliff Holton** (1950–67)	Arsenal, Watford Northampton, Crystal Palace, Charlton and Orient	292
5	**Ray Crawford** (1957–70)	Portsmouth, Ipswich, Wolves, West Brom Charlton and Colchester	289
=6	**Ronnie Allen** (1946–64)	Port Vale, West Brom and Crystal Palace	276
=6	**Ron Davies** (1959–75)	Chester, Luton Town, Norwich, Southampton, Porstmouth, Manchester United and Millwall	276
8	**Roger Hunt** (1959–71)	Liverpool and Bolton Wanderers	270
9	**Kevin Hector** (1962–82)	Bradford and Derby County	268
10	**Bryan Robson** (1964–)	Newcastle United, West Ham, Sunderland, Carlisle and Chelsea	260

GOALSCORERS – DIVISION ONE

		Goals	Season
1	**Jimmy Greaves** (Chelsea)	41	1960–61
2	**John Charles** (Leeds United)	38	1956–57
=3	**Ron Davies** (Southampton)	37	1966–67
	Jimmy Greaves (Spurs)	37	1962–63
	Dennis Westcott (Wolves)	37	1946–47
6	**Bobby Smith** (Spurs)	36	1957–58
7	**Jimmy Greaves** (Spurs)	35	1963–64
8	**Tommy Thompson** (Preston)	34	1957–58
=9	**Ray Crawford** (Ipswich)	33	1961–62
	Derek Kevan (West Brom)	33	1961–62
	Francis Lee (Manchester City)	33	1971–72
	Nat Lofthouse (Bolton Wanderers)	33	1955–56
	George Robledo (Newcastle United)	33	1951–52
	Ronnie Rooke (Arsenal)	33	1947–48
	Gordon Turner (Luton Town)	33	1957–58

GOALSCORERS – DIVISION TWO

		Goals	Season
1	**Derek Dooley** (Sheffield Wednesday)	46	1951–52
2	**Arthur Rowley** (Leicester City)	44	1956–57
3	**Tom Johnston** (Leyton Orient 35; Blackburn Rovers 8)	43	1957–58
=4	**Brian Clough** (Middlesbrough)	42	1958–59
	John Charles (Leed's United)	42	1953–54
6	**Roger Hunt** (Liverpool)	41	1961–62
7	**Brian Clough** (Middlesbrough)	40	1957–58
=8	**Brian Clough** (Middlesbrough)	39	1959–60
	Ray Crawford (Ipswich Town)	39	1960–61
	Arthur Rowley (Leicester City)	39	1952–53

GOALSCORERS – DIVISION THREE (FROM 1958–59)

		Goals	Season
1	**Derek Reeves** (Southampton)	39	1959–60
2	**Cliff Holton** (Northampton Town 36; Watford 1)	37	1961–62
=3	**Brian Bedford** (QPR)	36	1961–62
	Tony Richards (Walsall)	36	1960–61
=5	**Ted MacDougall** (Bournemouth)	35	1971–72
	Dixie McNeil (Hereford United)	35	1975–76
	Alf Wood (Shrewsbury Town)	35	1971–72
=8	**Ron Rafferty** (Grimsby Town)	34	1961–62
	Alan Buckley (Walsall)	34	1975–76
=10	**Brian Bedford** (QPR)	33	1960–61
	Roger Hunt (Grimsby Town)	33	1959–60
	Colin Taylor (Walsall)	33	1960–61

GOALSCORERS – DIVISION FOUR (FROM 1958–59)

		Goals	Season
1	**Terry Bly** (Peterborough United)	52	1960–61
2	**Kevin Hector** (Bradford)	44	1965–66
=3	**Ted MacDougall** (Bournemouth)	42	1970–71
	Cliff Holton (Watford)	42	1959–60
5	**Hugh McIlmoyle** (Carlisle)	39	1963–64
=6	**Bobby Hunt** (Colchester)	37	1961–62
	Arthur Rowley (Shrewsbury Town)	37	1958–59
=8	**Keith Edwards** (Sheffield United 35; Hull 1)	36	1981–82
	Alick Jeffrey (Doncaster Rovers)	36	1964–65
=10	**Terry Harkin** (Crewe Alexandra)	35	1964–65
	Craig Madden (Bury)	35	1981–82
	George Hudson (Accrington Stanley)	35	1960–61

ALL-TIME HONOURS

'Top Ten' lists of Division One Champions and FA Cup winners:

Division One Championship

1 Liverpool, 14
2 Arsenal, 8
=3 Aston Villa, 7
Everton, 7
Manchester United, 7
6 Sunderland, 6
=7 Newcastle United, 4
Sheffield Wednesday, 4
=9 Huddersfield Town, 3
Wolves, 3

FA Cup Final Wins

=1 Aston Villa, 7
Spurs, 7
=3 Blackburn Rovers, 6
Newcastle United, 6
=5 Arsenal, 5
Manchester United, 5
The Wanderers, 5
West Brom, 5
=9 Bolton Wanderers, 4
Manchester City, 4
Sheffield United, 4
Wolves, 4

TRANSFERS

'Top Ten' List of record transfers between English Football League clubs:

1	**Bryan Robson**	£1,500,000	West Brom to Manchester United, October 1981
2	**Andy Gray**	£1,469,000	Aston Villa to Wolves, September 1979
3	**Steve Daley**	£1,437,500	Wolves to Manchester City, September 1979
4	**Kenny Sansom**	£1,350,000	Crystal Palace to Arsenal, August 1980
=5	**Clive Allen**	£1,250,000	Arsenal to Crystal Palace, August 1980
	Garry Birtles	£1,250,000	Nottingham Forest to Manchester United, October 1980
	Kevin Reeves	£1,250,000	Norwich City, to Manchester City, March 1980
	Ian Wallace	£1,250,000	Coventry to Nottingham Forest, July 1980
=9	**Clive Allen**	£1,200,000	QPR to Arsenal, June 1980
	Trevor Francis	£1,200,000	Nottingham Forest to Manchester City, September 1981

TOP TEN ATTENDANCES

'Top Ten' all-time list of club record attendances for each of the Football League grounds:

1	**Maine Road**	84,569	Manchester City *v.* Stoke, FA Cup 6th round, 3 March 1934
2	**Stamford Bridge**	82,905	Chelsea *v.* Arsenal, Division One, 12 October 1935
3	**Goodison Park**	78,299	Everton *v.* Liverpool, Division One, 18 September 1948
4	**Villa Park**	76,588	Aston Villa *v.* Derby County, FA Cup 6th round, 2 March 1946
5	**Roker Park**	75,118	Sunderland *v.* Derby County, FA Cup 6th round replay, 8 March 1933
6	**White Hart Lane**	75,038	Spurs *v.* Sunderland, FA Cup 6th round, 5 March 1938
7	**The Valley**	75,031	Charlton Athletic *v.* Aston Villa, FA Cup 5th round, 12 February 1938
8	**Highbury**	73,295	Arsenal *v.* Sunderland, Division One, 9 March 1935
9	**Hillsborough**	72,841	Sheffield Wednesday *v.* Manchester City, FA Cup 5th round, 17 February 1934
10	**Old Trafford**	70,504	Manchester United *v.* Aston Villa, Division One, 27 December 1920

STAN MORTENSEN'S DREAM TEAM

1 Frank Swift
2 Eddie Shimwell
3 George Hardwick
4 Harry Johnston
5 Neil Franklin
6 Joe Mercer (capt)
7 Stan Matthews
8 Jimmy Hagan
9 Tommy Lawton
10 Wilf Mannion
11 Tom Finney
Sub: Jackie Milburn

'The hardest job was deciding which of my old team-mates to leave out. I was lucky enough to play with the very best and I could have selected three more teams of similar standard. In the end I plumped for the finest players in each position and I *know* it would have worked as a winning combination. I would have loved the chance to have played in this attack.'

Stan Mortensen was one of the greatest forwards ever to pull on an England shirt. He scored 23 goals in 25 matches in the immediate post-war years, netting four in his England debut against Portugal in 1947. A wartime bomber pilot who survived a terrifying crash, Morty will always be remembered for his historic hat-trick for Blackpool in the 1953 FA Cup Final at Wembley.